✮ Mel Bay Presents ✮

Ballads & Songs of the Civil War

By Jerry Silverman

Photo Credits

State Historical Society of Missouri, Columbia: Pages 5, 12, 20–21, 26–27, 38, 49, 65, 84, 85, 109, 125, 151, 161, 170, 171, 177,184, 195, 199, 201, 203, 209, 215, 223, 225, 227, 233, 247, 259, 267, 269, 272.

Chicago Historical Society: Page 221.

Contents

The Union

The Confederacy

Lincoln

Universal Sentiments

Soldiers' Songs

Battles

Negro Spirituals & Abolitionist Songs

The Lighter Side

Post Bellum

Introduction

The Civil War lasted almost four years to the day. It began on April 12, 1861, with the Confederate firing upon Fort Sumter, and ended with Lee's surrender to Grant at Appomattox on April 9, 1865. That terrible struggle, which cost over 600,000 American lives—Northern and Southern—has left us an incredibly rich musical legacy. Songs were written and sung by both sides on every aspect of the war: stirring marching songs, sentimental ballads, descriptions of battles and their aftermath, election campaign songs, songs with a political message, songs with a social conscience, minstrel songs, and satirical and humorous ditties.

Since both Northern and Southern song writers used the same language—musical as well as verbal—to express divergent as well as similar opinions and feelings, there is a certain homogeneity in a representative collection of ballads and songs of this period. The only body of songs which stands alone is the Negro spirituals; there obviously could not be a "separate but equal" black expression supporting slavery.

Ballads and songs of the Civil War are not cultural artifacts, frozen in time, to be placed under glass or studied through a microscope. They are real songs, made to be sung by real people. Their musical language is simple and direct. Their lyrics, while occasionally slipping into mid-19th century bombast, may still be sung by us today without embarrassment.

Mention must be made, however, of the use of pseudo–Negro dialect and what would certainly today be considered offensively racist terminology in a few of the songs. No historically accurate picture of the mentality of the time could be drawn by "cleaning up" that material. The decision as to how these songs should be performed is left to the present reader who may wish to sing them.

The best way to approach this book is seated at the piano or with guitar in hand. The musical arrangements have been kept technically simple—hopefully within the grasp of most amateur musicians. In singing and playing through them, a precious legacy of American history will once again come alive.

The Union

The Battle Cry of Freedom

(Rallying Song)

"The Battle Cry of Freedom" was first heard in Chicago on April 24, 1862. It was performed at a war rally, and was an instant success. Soon after, Union soldiers took up "the battle cry" and sang it with gusto throughout the war. The song retained its popularity after Appomattox, with its publishers, Root & Cady, claiming a sale of over 350,000 copies by 1867.

Words and music by George F. Root

Shout – ing the bat–tle cry of free — dom. The Un – ion for–ev – er, Hur–

rah, boys, hur–rah! Down with the trai – tor, Up with the star; While we

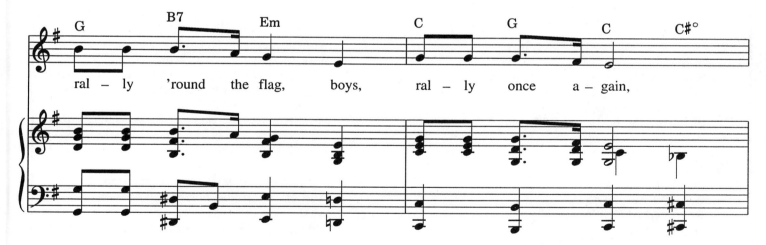

ral – ly 'round the flag, boys, ral – ly once a – gain,

Shout – ing the bat – tle cry of free — dom.

2. We are springing to the call of our brothers gone before,
   Shouting the battle cry of freedom,
   And we'll fill the vacant ranks with a million freemen more,
   Shouting the battle cry of freedom. *Chorus*

3. We will welcome to our numbers the loyal, true, and brave,
   Shouting the battle cry of freedom,
   And although they may be poor not a man shall be a slave,
   Shouting the battle cry of freedom. *Chorus*

4. So we're springing to the call from the East and from the West,
   Shouting the battle cry of freedom,
   And we'll hurl the Rebel crew from the land we love the best,
   Shouting the battle cry of freedom. *Chorus*

The Battle Cry of Freedom, II

(Battle Song)

Words and music by George F. Root

1. We are marching to the field, boys,
   We're going to the fight,
     Shouting the battle cry of freedom,
   And we bear the glorious stars
   For the Union and the right,
     Shouting the battle cry of freedom.

Chorus:
   The Union forever!
   Hurrah! Boys, hurrah!
   Down with the traitor,
   Up with the star.
   For we're marching to the field, boys,
   Going to the fight,
   Shouting the battle cry of freedom.

2. We will meet the Rebel host, boys,
   With fearless heart and true,
     Shouting the battle cry of freedom,
   And we'll show what Uncle Sam has
   For loyal men to do,
     Shouting the battle cry of freedom. *Chorus*

3. If we fall amid the fray, boys,
   We'll face them to the last,
     Shouting the battle cry of freedom,
   And our comrades brave shall hear us
   As they go rushing past,
     Shouting the battle cry of freedom. *Chorus*

4. Yes, for Liberty and Union
   We're springing to the fight,
     Shouting the battle cry of freedom,
   And the vict'ry shall be ours
   For we're rising in our might,
     Shouting the battle cry of freedom. *Chorus*

Southern Battle Cry of Freedom

Words: anonymous
Music: "Battle Cry of Freedom" (by George F. Root)

1. We are marching to the field, boys,
   We're going to the fight,
     Shouting the battle cry of freedom.
   And we bear the Heavenly cross,
   For our cause is in the right,
     Shouting the battle cry of freedom.

Chorus:
   Our rights forever,
   Hurrah! Boys! Hurrah!
   Down with the tyrants,
   Raise the Southern star,
   And we'll rally 'round the flag, boys,
   We'll rally once again,
   Shouting the battle cry of freedom.

2. We'll meet the Yankee hosts, boys,
   With fearless hearts and true,
     Shouting the battle cry of freedom,
   And we'll show the dastard minions,
   What Southern pluck can do,
     Shouting the battle cry of freedom. *Chorus*

3. We'll fight them to the last, boys,
   If we fall in the strife,
     Shouting the battle cry of freedom,
   Our comrades – noble boys!
   Will avenge us, life for life,
     Shouting the battle cry of freedom. *Chorus*

9

The Battle Hymn of the Republic

Julia Ward Howe wrote the words to "The Battle Hymn of the Republic" during a visit to army encampments near Washington in November 1861. True to the spirit of the times, she set her lyrics to the melody of a well-known song, "John Brown's Body."

Words by Julia Ward Howe
Music: "John Brown's Body"

Mine eyes have seen the glo - ry of the com - ing of the Lord; He is tram - pling out the vin - tage where the grapes of wrath are stored; He hath loosed the fate - ful light - ning of His ter - ri - ble swift sword, His truth is march - ing on.

John Brown's Body

"Now, if it is deemed necessary that I should forfeit my life for the furtherance of the ends of justice, and mingle my blood further with the blood of my children and with the blood of millions in this slave country whose rights are disregarded by wicked, cruel, and unjust enactments, I say, let it be done." (*John Brown addressing the court at his trial*)

He was hanged on December 2, 1859.

Words: anonymous
Music: "Say, Brothers, Will You Meet Us?" (ascribed to William Steffe)

1. John Brown's body lies a-mouldering in the grave,
   John Brown's body lies a-mouldering in the grave,
   John Brown's body lies a-mouldering in the grave,
   But his soul goes marching on.

Chorus:
   Glory, glory, hallelujah,
   Glory, glory, hallelujah,
   Glory, glory, hallelujah,
   His soul goes marching on.

2. He's gone to be a soldier in the Army of the Lord…
   His soul goes marching on. *Chorus*

3. John Brown's knapsack is strapped upon his back…
   His soul goes marching on. *Chorus*

4. John Brown died that the slaves might be free…
   But his soul goes marching on. *Chorus*

5. The stars above in Heaven now are looking kindly down…
   On the grave of old John Brown. *Chorus*

John Brown

ALL QUIET

ALONG THE

POTOMAC

TO-NIGHT.

BALTIMORE:

Published by MILLER & BEACHAM, No. 10 North Charles Street.

"ALL QUIET ALONG THE POTOMAC TO-NIGHT."

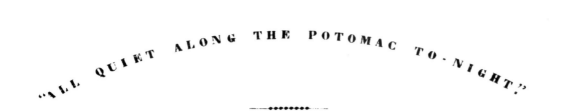

MODERATO.

"All

qui - et a - long the Po - to - mac to-night," Ex - cept here and there a stray picket   Is

shot   as he walks on his beat to   and fro,   By a   ri - fleman hid in the   thicket;   'Tis

63

2

"All quiet along the Potomac to-night,"
    Where the soldiers lie peacefully dreaming,
And their tents in the rays of the clear autumn moon,
    And the light of the camp fires are gleaming;
There's only the sound of the lone sentry's tread,
    As he tramps from the rock to the fountain,
And thinks of the two on the low trundle bed
    Far away in the cot on the mountain.

3

His musket falls slack— his face, dark and grim,
    Grows gentle with memories tender,
As he mutters a pray'r for the children asleep,
    And their mother "May heaven defend her!"
The moon seems to shine as brightly as then—
    That night, when the love yet unspoken
Leap'd up to his lips, and when low murmur'd vows
    Were pledg'd, to be ever unbroken.

4

Then drawing his sleeve roughly o'er his eyes,
    He dashes off the tears that are welling,
And gathers his gun close up to his breast,
    As if to keep down the heart's swelling;
He passes the fountain, the blasted pine tree,
    And his footstep is lagging and weary,
Yet onward he goes, thro' the broad belt of light,
    Toward the shades of the forest so dreary.

5

Hark! was it the night-wind that rustles the leaves!
    Was it the moonlight so wond'rously flashing?
It look'd like a rifle! "Ha, Mary good bye!"
    And his life-blood is ebbing and plashing.
"All quiet along the Potomac to-night,"
    No sound save the rush of the river;
While soft falls the dew on the face of the dead,
    "The Picket's" off duty for ever.

Clayton

The John Brown Song

Words: anonymous
Music: "John Brown's Body"

1. Old John Brown's body lies a-mouldering in the grave,
   While weep the sons of bondage whom he ventured all to save;
   But though he lost his life in struggling for the slave,
   His truth is marching on.

Chorus
   Glory, glory, hallelujah!
   Glory, glory, hallelujah!
   Glory, glory, hallelujah!
   His truth is marching on!

2. John Brown was a hero, undaunted, true, and brave;
   Kansas knew his valor when he fought her rights to save;
   And now though the grass grows green above his grave,
   His truth is marching on. *Chorus*

3. He captured Harper's Ferry with his nineteen men so few,
   And he frightened "Old Virginny" till she trembled through and through,
   They hung him for a traitor, themselves a traitor crew,
   But his truth is marching on. *Chorus*

4. John Brown was John the Baptist for the Christ we are to see,
   Christ who of the bondsman shall the Liberator be;
   And soon throughout the sunny South the slaves shall all be free.
   For his truth is marching on. *Chorus*

5. The conflict that he heralded, he looks from heaven to view,
   On the army of the Union with its flag, red, white, and blue,
   And heaven shall ring with anthems o'er the deeds they mean to do,
   For his truth is marching on. *Chorus*

6. Oh, soldiers of freedom, then strike while strike you may
   The deathblow of oppression in a better time and way;
   For the dawn of old John Brown has brightened into day,
   And his truth is marching on. *Chorus*

Marching Song of the First Arkansas (Negro) Regiment

The Militia Act of July 17, 1862, authorized the enrollment of "persons of the African descent" in "any military or naval service for which they may be found competent." Captain Lindley Miller was a white officer of the First Arkansas Colored Regiment.

Words ascribed to Capt. Lindley Miller
Music: "John Brown's Body"

1. Oh, we're the bully soldiers of the "First of Arkansas,"
   We are fighting for the Union, we are fighting for the law,
   We can hit a Rebel further than a white man ever saw,
   As we go marching on.

   Chorus
   Glory, glory, hallelujah,
   Glory, glory, hallelujah,
   Glory, glory, hallelujah,
   As we go marching on.

2. See, there above the center, where the flag is waving bright,
   We are going out of slavery; we're bound for freedom's light;
   We mean to show Jeff Davis how the Africans can fight,
   As we go marching on! *Chorus*

3. We have done with hoeing cotton, we have done with hoeing corn,
   We are colored Yankee soldiers, now, as sure as you are born;
   When the masters hear us yelling, they'll think it's Gabriel's horn,
   As we go marching on. *Chorus*

4. They will have to pay us wages, the wages of their sin,
   They will have to bow their foreheads to their colored kith and kin,
   They will have to give us house-room, or the roof shall tumble in!
   As we go marching on. *Chorus*

5. We heard the Proclamation, master hush it as he will,
   The bird he sing it to us, hoppin' on the cotton hill,
   And the possum up the gum tree, he couldn't keep it still,
   As he went climbing on. *Chorus*

6. They said, "now colored brethren, you shall be forever free,
   From the first of January, Eighteen hundred sixty-three."
   We heard it in the river going rushing to the sea,
   As it went sounding on. *Chorus*

7. Father Abraham has spoken and the message has been sent,
   The prison doors he opened, and out the pris'ners went,
   To join the sable army of the "African descent,"
   As we go marching on. *Chorus*

8. Then fall in, colored brethren, you'd better do it soon,
   Don't you hear the drum a-beating the Yankee Doodle tune?
   We are with you now this morning, we'll be far away at noon,
   As we go marching on. *Chorus*

Give Us a Flag

This is the regimental song of the Massachusetts Fifty-Fourth (Colored) Regiment. It was organized in early 1863 with volunteers not only from Massachusetts (since there were not enough Negroes living in that state to complete the ranks) but from every state in the Union, as well as Canada. The 54th saw action for the first time in the assault on Fort Wagner at the entrance to Charleston harbor. They took very heavy casualties and were driven back, but (July 18, 1863) they proved to the doubters in the North as well as the South that they could fight with the best of them.

Words: anonymous
Music: "Hoist Up the Flag" (by Billy Holmes)

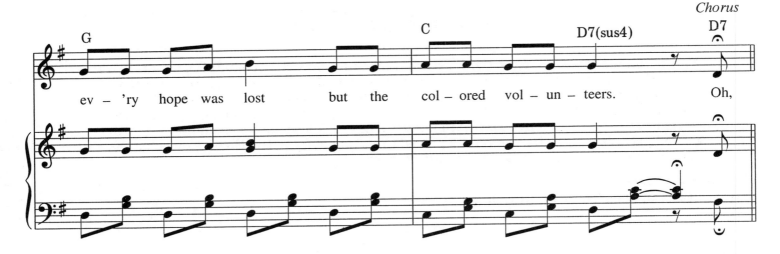

Chorus

ev – 'ry hope was lost but the col – ored vol – un – teers. Oh,

give us a flag, all free with – out a slave; We'll

fight to de – fend it as our fa – thers did so brave; The

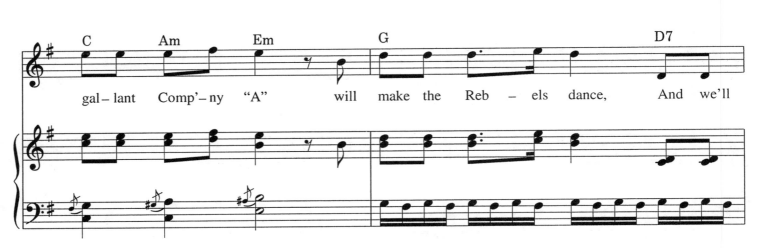

gal – lant Comp'–ny "A" will make the Reb – els dance, And we'll

stand by the Un – ion if we on – ly have a chance.

2. McClellan went to Richmond with two hundred thousand brave;
   He said, "Keep back the niggers" and the Union he would save.
   Little Mac he had his way, still the Union is in tears,
   NOW they call for the help of the colored volunteers. *Chorus*

3. Old Jeff says he'll hang us if we dare to meet him armed,
   A very big thing, but we are not at all alarmed;
   For he first has got to catch us before the way is clear,
   And that is "what's the matter" with the colored volunteer. *Chorus*

4. So rally, boys, rally, let us never mind the past;
   We had a hard road to travel, but our day is coming fast;
   For God is the right, and we have no need to fear,
   The Union must be saved by the colored volunteer. *Chorus*

5. Then here is to the 54th, which has been nobly tried,
   They were willing, they were ready, with their bayonets by their side,
   Colonel Shaw led them on and he had no cause to fear,
   About the courage of the colored volunteer. *Chorus*

For the Dear Old Flag I Die

Stephen Foster's name is usually associated with his bucolic, if somewhat fanciful, visions of "the Old South" as pictured in his "Old Black Joe" and "Old Folks at Home." Yet, he too was moved by the horror and the reality of the conflict to collaborate on this sentimental ballad.

Words by George Cooper
Music by Stephen Collins Foster

face,   Moth – er   take   me   to   your   heart,   Let   me

die   in   your   em ___ brace.   For the   dear   old   Flag   I

die,   Moth – er,   dry   your   weep – ing   eye;   For the

hon – or   of   our   land   And   the   dear   old   Flag   I   die."

19

2. "Do not mourn, my mother, dear,
   Every pang will soon be o'er;
   For I hear the angel band
   Calling from their starry shore;
   Now I see their banners wave
   In the light of perfect day,
   Though 'tis hard to part with you,
   Yet I would not wish to stay." *Chorus*

3. Farewell mother, Death's cold hand
   Weighs upon my spirit now,
   And I feel his blighting breath
   Fan my pallid cheek and brow.
   Closer! closer! to your heart,
   Let me feel that you are by,
   While my sight is growing dim,
   For the dear old Flag I die. *Chorus*

Marching Along

At 2:00 A.M. on July 21, 1862—the morning after the Union rout at Bull Run—George C. McLellan received a telegram summoning him to take command of the fledgling Army of the Potomac. In reviewing his troops, McLellan found "no army to command—only a mere collection of regiments cowering on the banks of the Potomac...." He was soon to bring order out of the chaos and instill a true fighting spirit in his men.

Words and Music by William B. Bradbury

The ar – my is gath – 'ring from near and from far; The trum – pet is sound – ing the call for the war; Mc – Clel – lan's our lead – er, he's gal – lant and strong; We'll gird on our ar – mor and be march–ing a–long.

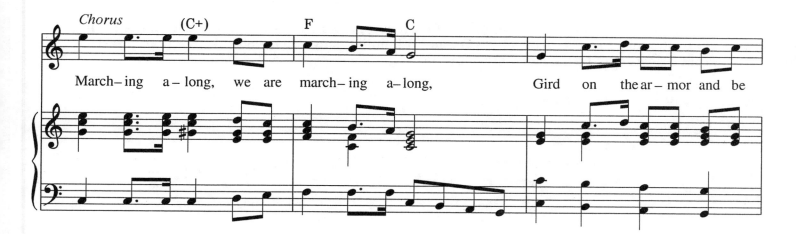

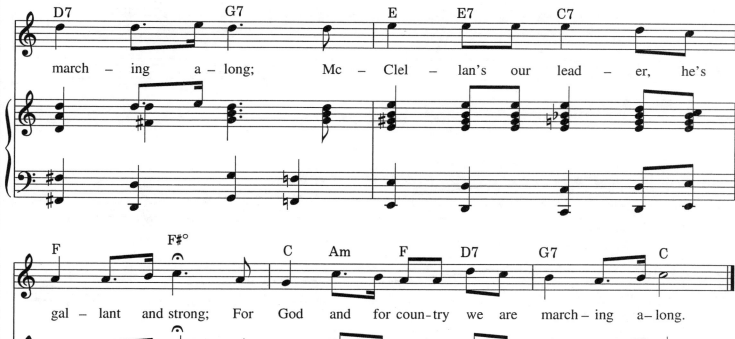

2. The foe is before us in battle array,
    But let us not waver or turn from the way;
    The Lord is our strength and the Union's our song;
    With courage and faith we are marching along. *Chorus*

3. Our wives and our children we leave in your care,
    We feel you will help them with sorrow to bear;
    'Tis hard thus to part, but we hope 'twon't be long,
    We'll keep up our heart as we're marching along. *Chorus*

4. We sigh for our country, we mourn for our dead,
    For them now our last drop of blood we will shed;
    Our cause is the right one – our foe's in the wrong;
    Then gladly we'll sing as we're marching along. *Chorus*

5. The flag of our country is floating on high,
    We'll stand by that flag till we conquer or die;
    McClellan's our leader, he's gallant and strong,
    We'll gird on our armor and be marching along. *Chorus*

The Army of the Free

The many soldiers in the Union Army of Irish descent would have certainly known the Irish patriotic song "The Wearing of the Green." A familiar, singable melody always guaranteed that a new set of lyrics would get a fair hearing.

Words by Frank H. Norton
Music: "The Wearing of the Green"

In the ar — my of the Un — ion we are march — ing in the van, And will do the work be — fore us, if the brav — est sol — diers can; We will drive the Reb — el forc — es from their strong — holds to the sea, And will

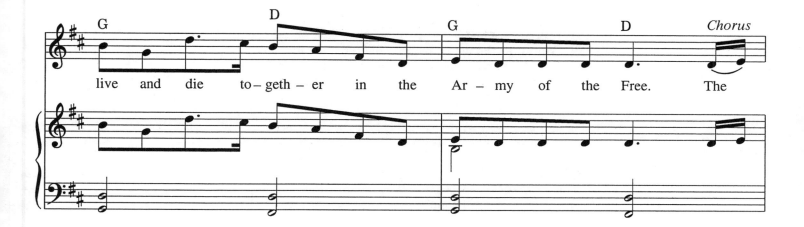

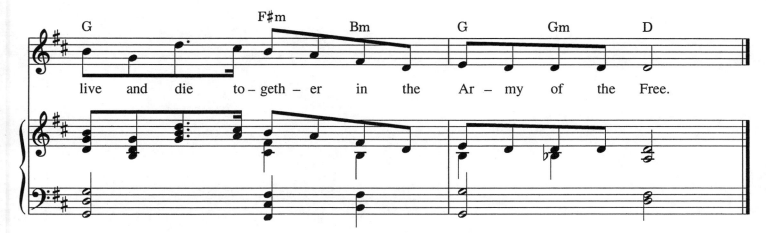

2. We may rust beneath inaction, we may sink beneath disease,
   The summer sun may scorch us or the winter's blasts may freeze,
   But whatever may befall us, we will let the Rebels see,
   That unconquered we shall remain the Army of the Free.
     The Army of the Free, the Army of the Free,
     Unconquered we shall still remain the Army of the Free.

3. We are the best division of a half a million souls,
   And only resting on our arms till the war cry onward rolls;
   When our gallant General Porter calls, why ready we shall be,
   To follow him forever with the Army of the Free.
     The Army of the Free, the Army of the Free,
     We will follow him forever with the Army of the Free.

4. We have Butterfield the daring and we've Martindale the cool,
   Where could we learn the art of war within a better school;
   Add Morell to the list of names, and we must all agree,
   We have the finest Generals in the Army of the Free.
     The Army of the Free, the Army of the Free,
     We have the finest Generals in the Army of the Free.

5. Though we live in winter quarters now, we're waiting but the hour,
   When Porter's brave division shall go forth in all its power,
   And when on the field of battle, fighting we shall be,
   We'll show that we cannot disgrace the Army of the Free.
     The Army of the Free, the Army of the Free,
     We'll show that we cannot disgrace the Army of the Free.

6. Then hurrah for our Division, may it soon be called to go,
   To add its strength to those who have advanced to meet the foe;
   God bless it, for we know right well, wherever it may be,
   'Twill never fail to honor our great Army of the Free.
     The Army of the Free, the Army of the Free,
     'Twill never fail to honor our great Army of the Free.

Tramp! Tramp! Tramp!

(The Prisoner's Hope)

George Root managed to express the "prisoner's hope" in such up-beat terms that it became a favorite marching song for the troops.

Words and music by George F. Root

2. In the battle front we stood,
   When their fiercest charge they made,
   And they swept us off a hundred men or more,
   But before we reached their lines,
   They were beaten back dismayed,
   And we heard the cry of vict'ry o'er and o'er.
   Chorus

3. So within the prison cell
   We are waiting for the day
   That shall come to open wide the iron door,
   And the hollow eye grows bright,
   And the poor heart almost gay,
   As we think of seeing home and friends once more.
   Chorus

Tramp! Tramp! Tramp!, II

(Southern Version)

Words: anonymous
Music by George F. Root

1. In my prison cell I sit,
   Thinking, mother, dear, of you,
   And my happy Southern home so far away;
   And my eyes they fill with tears
   'Spite of all that I can do,
   Though I try to cheer my comrades and be gay.

Chorus:
   Tramp! Tramp! Tramp!
   The boys are marching;
   Cheer up, comrades, they will come.
   And beneath the stars and bars
   We shall breathe the air again
   Of freemen in our own beloved home.

2. In the battle front we stood
   When their fiercest charge they made,
   And our soldiers by the thousands sank to die;
   But before they reached our lines,
   They were driven back dismayed,
   And the "Rebel yell" went upward to the sky. *Chorus*

3. Now our great commander Lee
   Crosses broad Potomac's stream,
   And his legions marching northward take their way.
   On Pennsylvania's roads
   Will their trusty muskets gleam,
   And her iron hills shall echo to the fray. *Chorus*

4. In the cruel stockade-pen
   Dying slowly day by day,
   For weary months we've waited all in vain;
   But if God will speed the way
   Of our gallant boys in gray,
   I shall see your face, dear mother, yet again. *Chorus*

5. When I close my eyes in sleep,
   All the dear ones 'round me come,
   At night my little sister to me calls;
   And mocking visions bring
   All the warm delights of home,
   While we freeze and starve in Northern prison walls.
   Chorus

6. So the weary days go by,
   And we wonder as we sigh,
   If with sight of home we'll never more be blessed.
   Our hearts within us sink,
   And we murmur, though we try
   To leave it all with Him who knowest best. *Chorus*

Nine Miles to the Junction

On April 11, 1861, Governor William Sprague of Rhode Island addressed a letter to President Lincoln: "...I should not now be correctly representing the public sentiment of the people of this state, did I not assure you of their loyalty to the government of the Union, and of their anxiety to do their utmost to maintain it...." By April 23, a regiment of 1,400 Rhode Islanders had reached Annapolis by steamer from New York. From Annapolis they took up their line of march for Washington, and encamped in a grove near the city until the Army of the Potomac advanced in March 1862. It bore the name of "Camp Sprague."

The governor remained with the Rhode Island troops most of the time, and participated in the battle of Bull Run (July 16, 1861). "He was everywhere in the thickest of the fight; and when his horse was shot out from under him by a musket ball, the governor immediately procured another animal and still continued conspicuous upon the field, encouraging the men by his presence and bravery. The two bullet-holes found in his clothes, after the battle, show that he did not shun danger." (***Memoirs Of Rhode Island Officers Who Were Engaged In The Service Of Their Country During The Great Rebellion Of The South,*** *Providence, 1867*)

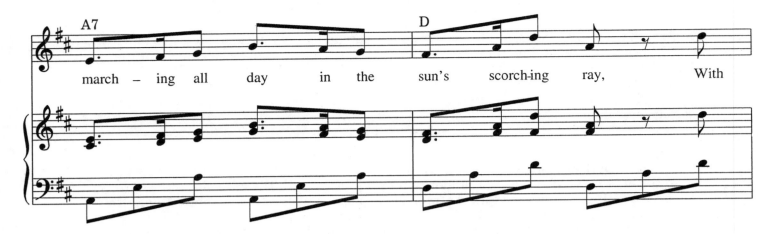

march – ing all day in the sun's scorch-ing ray, With

two bis – cuits each as a ra – tion, When we asked Gov-'nor Sprague to ___

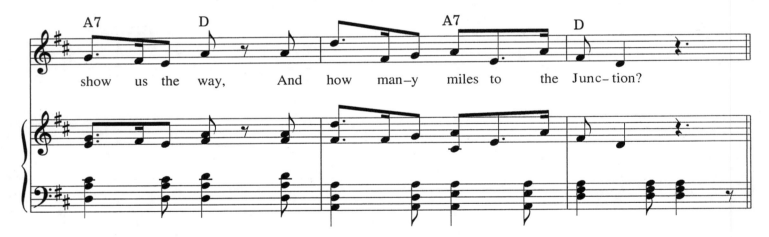

show us the way, And how man–y miles to the Junc–tion?

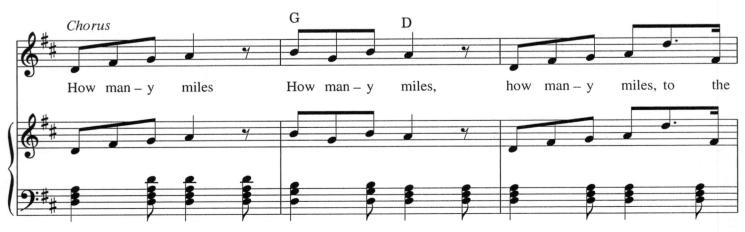

Chorus

How man – y miles How man – y miles, how man – y miles, to the

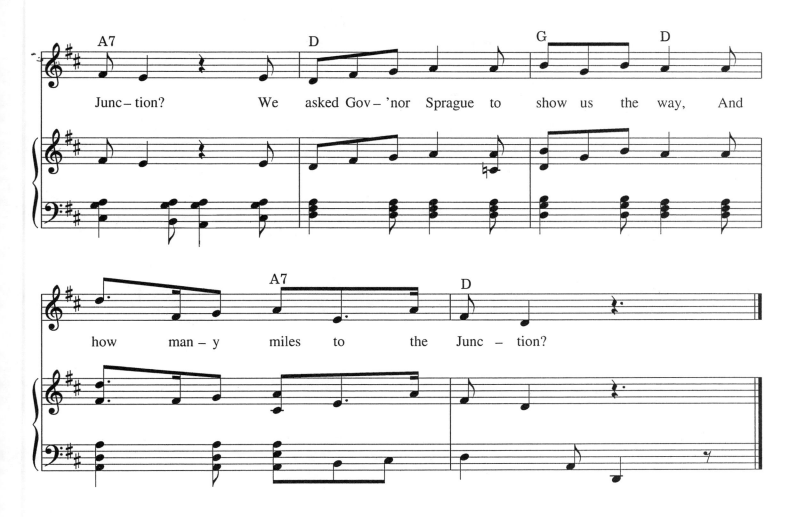

Junc – tion? We asked Gov – 'nor Sprague to show us the way, And how man – y miles to the Junc – tion?

2. And Rhode Island boys cheered us on out of sight,
   After giving the following injunction:
   "Just keep up your courage, you'll get there tonight,
   For it's only nine miles to the Junction."
   They gave us hot coffee, a grasp of the hand,
   Which cheered and refreshed our exhaustion,
   And we reached in six hours the long-promised land,
   For 'twas only nine miles to the Junction.
     Only nine miles, only nine miles,
     Only nine miles to the Junction.
     We reached in six hours the long-promised land,
     For 'twas only nine miles to the Junction.

3. And now as we meet them in Washington's streets,
   They always do hail us with unction,
   And still the old cry someone surely repeats:
   "It's only nine miles to the Junction!"
   Three cheers for the warm-hearted Rhode Island boys,
   May each one be true to his function,
   And whenever we meet, let us each other greet
   With, "Only nine miles to the Junction!"
     Only nine miles, only nine miles,
     Only nine miles to the Junction,
     Whenever we meet, let us each other greet,
     With, "Only nine miles to the Junction!"

4. Nine cheers for the flag under which we will fight,
   If the traitors should dare to assail it,
   One cheer for each mile that we made on that night,
   When 'twas only nine miles to me Junction.
   With hearts thus united, our breasts to the foe,
   Once again with delight we will hail it,
   And if duty should call us, still onward we'll go,
   If even nine miles to the Junction.
     Even nine miles, even nine miles,
     Even nine miles to the Junction.
     If duty should call, still onward we'll go,
     If even nine miles to the Junction.

The Why and the Wherefore

speak my mind quite free — ly — Now ree — — ly."

2. "Why, why, why, and why,
   And why to the war, young man?"
   "Did a man ever fight for a holier cause,
   Than Freedom and Flag and Equal Laws?
   Just speak your mind quite freely - Now reely."

3. "Which, which, which, and which,
   And which is the Flag of the free?"
   "O Washington's Flag, with the stripes and the stars,
   Will you give such a name to the thing with the bars?
   I speak my mind quite freely - Now reely."

4. "Who, who, who, and who,
   And who goes with you to the war?"
   "Ten thousand brave lads, and if they should stay here,
   The girls would cry shame, and *they'd* volunteer!
   They speak their mind quite freely - Now reely."

5. "When, when, when, and when,
   And when do you mean to come back?"
   "When Rebellion is crushed and the Union restored,
   And Freedom is safe - yes, then, please the Lord!
   I speak my mind quite freely - Now reely."

6. "What, what, what, and what,
   And what will you gain by that?"
   "O I've gained enough whatever the cost,
   If Freedom, the hope of the world, isn't lost.
   I speak my mind quite freely - Now reely."

Marching Through Georgia

"I could cut a swath through to the sea, divide the Confederacy in two, and come up on the rear of Lee." (*General William T. Sherman to Grant, November 1864*)

Words and music by Henry C. Work

fif–ty thou–sand strong, While we were march–ing through Geor – gia. Hur –

rah! Hur–rah! We bring the ju – bi – lee! Hur – rah! Hur rah! The

flag that makes you free! So we sang the cho – rus from At –

lan–ta to the sea, While we were march – ing through Geor – gia.

2. How the darkeys shouted when they heard the joyful sound!
   How the turkeys gobbled which our commissary found!
   How the sweet potatoes even started from the ground,
     While we were marching through Georgia.   *Chorus*

3. Yes, and there were Union men who wept with joyful tears,
   When they saw the honored flag they had not seen for years;
   Hardly could they be restrained from breaking forth in cheers,
     While we were marching through Georgia.   *Chorus*

4. "Sherman's dashing Yankee boys will never reach the coast!"
   So the saucy Rebels said, and 'twas a handsome boast;
   Had they not forgot, alas! to reckon with the host,
     While we were marching through Georgia.   *Chorus*

5. So we made a thoroughfare for Freedom and her train,
   Sixty miles in latitude, three hundred to the main;
   Treason fled before us, for resistance was in vain,
     While we were marching through Georgia.   *Chorus*

The Confederacy

Dixie's Land

Daniel Decatur Emmett's "Dixie's Land" was premiered to tumultuous success by Emmett himself in a minstrel show in New York in September 1859. Despite its Northern "blackface" origins, it was unhesitatingly adopted by the Confederacy, where it became its rallying song, marching song, and anthem rolled into one. It nevertheless retained its popularity in the North, in its original form, and in numerous parodied versions. Lincoln counted it among his favorites, and called for it when being serenaded by a military band a few days after the close of the war.

Words and music by Daniel D. Emmett

wish I was in de land ob cot–ton, Old times dar am not for-got-ten, Look a–

way! Look a– way! Look a– way! Dix–ie Land. In

Dix – ie Land__ whar__ I was born in, Ear – ly on one frost – y morn–in', Look a–

Chorus

way! Look a – way! Look a - way! Dix – ie Land. Den__ I

wish I was in Dix – ie, Hoo – ray! Hoo – ray! In____

Dix – ie Land I'll take my stand, To lib and die in Dix – ie, A –

2. Ole missus marry "Will de weaber,"
   Willium was a gay deceaber;
     Look away! Look away!
     Look away! Dixie Land.
   But when he put his arm around 'er.
   He smiled as fierce as a forty pounder,
     Look away! Look away!
     Look away! Dixie Land.   *Chorus*

3. His face was sharp as a butcher's cleaber,
   But dat did not seem to greab 'er;
     Look away, etc.
   Ole missus acted de foolish part,
   And died for a man dat broke her heart,
     Look away, etc.   *Chorus*

4. Now here's a health to the next old Missus,
   An' all de gals dat want to kiss us;
     Look away, etc.
   But if you want to drive 'way sorrow,
   Come and hear dis song tomorrow,
     Look away, etc.   *Chorus*

5. Dar's buckwheat cakes and Injun batter,
   Makes you fat or a little fatter;
     Look away, etc.
   Den hoe it down an' scratch your grabble,
   To Dixie's Land I'm bound to trabble,
     Look away, etc.   *Chorus*

Dixie

Words by Albert Pike
Music: "Dixie's Land" (by Daniel D. Emmett)

1. Southrons, hear your country call you!
   Up, lest worse than death befall you!
   To arms! To arms! To arms! In Dixie!
   Lo! all the beacon fires are lighted
   Let all hearts be now united!
   To arms! To arms! To arms! In Dixie!

   Chorus:
   Advance the flag of Dixie!
   Hurrah! Hurrah!
   For Dixie's Land we take our stand,
   And live or die for Dixie!
   To arms! To arms!
   And conquer peace for Dixie!
   To arms! To arms!
   And conquer peace for Dixie!

2. Hear the Northern thunders mutter!
   Northern flags in South winds flutter!
   To arms! etc.
   Send them back your fierce defiance!
   Stamp upon the cursed alliance!
   To arms! etc. *Chorus*

3. Fear no danger! Shun no labor!
   Lift up rifle, pike, and sabre!
   To arms! etc.
   Shoulder pressing close to shoulder,
   Let the odds make each heart bolder!
   To arms! etc. *Chorus*

4. How the South's great heart rejoices
   At your cannon's ringing voices!
   To arms! etc.
   For faith betrayed and pledges broken,
   Wrongs inflicted, insults spoken,
   To arms! etc. *Chorus*

5. Strong as lions, swift as eagles,
   Back to their kennels hunt these beagles!
   To arms! etc.
   Cut the unequal bond asunder!
   Let them hence each other plunder!
   To arms! etc. *Chorus*

6. Swear upon your country's altar
   Never to submit or falter!
   To arms! etc.
   Till the spoilers are defeated,
   Till the Lord's work is completed,
   To arms! etc. *Chorus*

7. Halt not till our Federation
   Secures among earth's powers its station!
   To arms! etc.
   Then at peace, and crowned with glory,
   Hear your children tell the story!
   To arms! etc. *Chorus*

8. If the loved ones weep in sadness,
   Victory soon shall bring them gladness,
   To arms! etc.
   Exultant pride soon banish sorrow;
   Smiles chase tears away tomorrow.
   To arms! etc. *Chorus*

The Bonnie Blue Flag

Like Daniel Emmett, Harry McCarthy was a song writer and performer. However, McCarthy actually sang his "Bonnie Blue Flag" in concerts in the South before soldier audiences. It soon rivaled "Dixie" in popularity, spreading through the ranks in its original and its many parodied versions.

Words by Harry McCarthy
Music: "The Irish Jaunting Car"

toil; _____ And when our rights were threat-ened, the

cry rose near and far: _____ "Hur – rah for the

Bon – nie Blue Flag that bears a sin – gle star!" _____ Hur –

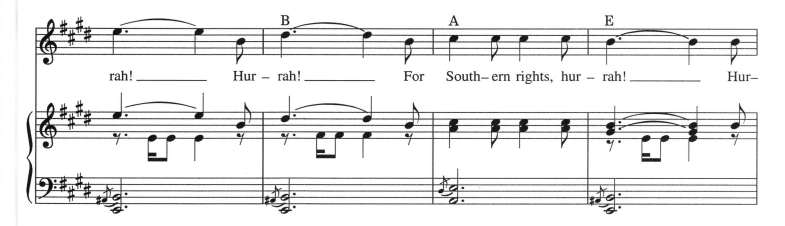

rah! _____ Hur – rah! _____ For South–ern rights, hur – rah! _____ Hur–

45

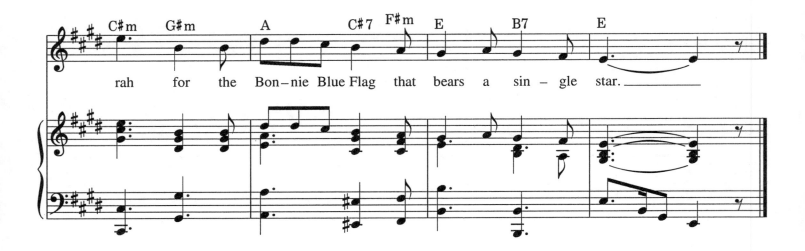

rah for the Bon—nie Blue Flag that bears a sin — gle star.

2. As long as the Union was faithful to her trust,
   Like friends and brethren, kind were we, and just;
   But now, when Northern treachery attempts our rights to mar,
   We hoist on high the Bonnie Blue Flag that bears a single star. *Chorus*

3. First gallant South Carolina nobly made the stand,
   Then came Alabama and took her by the hand;
   Next, quickly Mississippi, Georgia, and Florida,
   All raised on high the Bonnie Flag that bears a single star. *Chorus*

4. Ye men of valor gather round the banner of the right,
   Texas and fair Louisiana join us in the fight;
   Davis, our loved President, and Stephens statesmen are;
   Now rally round the Bonnie Blue Flag that bears a single star. *Chorus*

5. And here's to brave Virginia, the Old Dominion State.
   With the young Confederacy at length has linked her fate.
   Impelled by her example, now other States prepare
   To hoist on high the Bonnie Blue Flag that bears a single star. *Chorus*

6. Then here's to our Confederacy, strong we are and brave,
   Like patriots of old we'll fight, our heritage to save;
   And rather than submit to shame, to die we would prefer,
   So cheer for the Bonnie Blue Flag that bears a single star. *Chorus*

7. Then cheer, boys, cheer, raise a joyous shout,
   For Arkansas and North Carolina now have both gone out;
   And let another rousing cheer for Tennessee be given,
   The single star of the Bonnie Blue Flag has grown to be eleven. *Chorus*

The Yellow Rose of Texas

This rousing minstrel song predates the Civil War by at least eight years, having been published in 1853. The fact that, like "Dixie," it was of Northern origin did not prevent Confederate soldiers from adopting it as their own.

Spirited march ♩ = 120

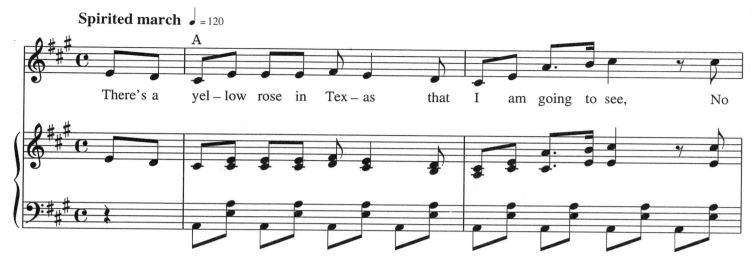

There's a yel – low rose in Tex – as that I am going to see, No

oth – er sol – dier knows her, no sol – dier, on – ly me; She

cried so when I left her, it like to broke my heart, And

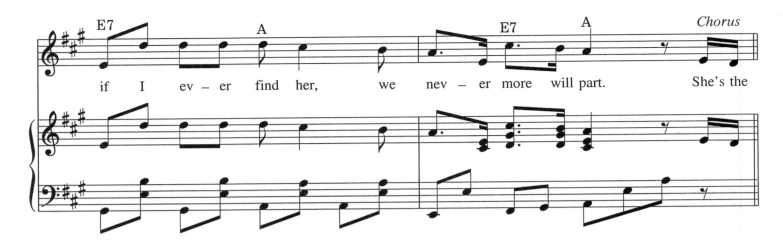

if I ev – er find her, we nev – er more will part. She's the

sweet – est rose of col – or this sol – dier ev – er knew, Her

eyes are bright as dia – monds, they spar – kle like the dew; You may

talk a – bout your dear – est May and sing of Ro – sa Lee, But the

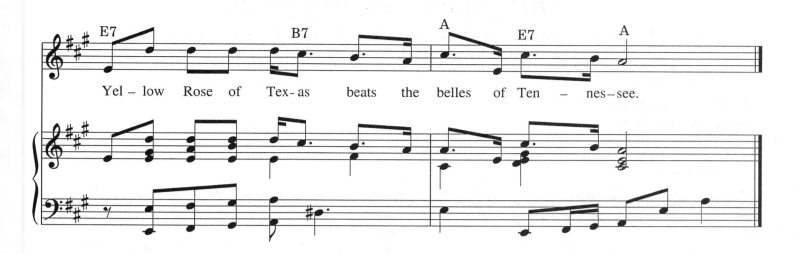

Yel – low Rose of Tex- as   beats   the   belles   of   Ten – nes – see.

2. Where the Rio Grande is flowing and the starry skies are bright,
   She walks along the river in the quiet summer night;
   She thinks if I remember, when we parted long ago,
   I promised to come back again and not to leave her so. *Chorus*

3. Oh, now I'm going to find her, for my heart is full of woe,
   And we'll sing the song together, that we sung so long ago;
   We'll play the banjo gaily, and we'll sing the songs of yore,
   And the Yellow Rose of Texas shall be mine forevermore. *Chorus*

Maryland, My Maryland

James R. Randall hoped that his stirring poem would help tip Maryland into the Confederacy. The poem itself was very well received, and when set to the familiar German air "Tannenbaum," it achieved the heights of popularity. Maryland, however, remained in the Union.

Words by James R. Randall
Music: "Tannenbaum"

flecked the streets of Bal – ti – more, And be the bat – tle queen of yore, Ma – ry – land, my Ma – ry – land!

2. Hark to an exiled son's appeal,
   Maryland, my Maryland!
   My Mother State, to thee I kneel,
   Maryland, my Maryland!
   For life or death, for woe or weal,
   Thy peerless chivalry reveal,
   And gird thy beauteous limbs with steel,
   Maryland, my Maryland!

3. Thou wilt not cower in the dust,
   Maryland, my Maryland!
   Thy beaming sword shall never rust,
   Maryland, my Maryland!
   Remember Carroll's sacred trust,
   And all thy slumberers with the just,
   Maryland, my Maryland!

4. Come! 'tis the red dawn of the day,
   Maryland, my Maryland!
   Come! with thy panoplied array,
   Maryland, my Maryland!
   With Ringgold's spirit for the fray,
   With Watson's blood at Monterey,
   With fearless Lowe and dashing May,
   Maryland, my Maryland!

5. Dear mother, burst the tyrant's chain,
   Maryland, my Maryland!
   Virginia should not call in vain,
   Maryland, my Maryland!
   She meets her sisters on the plain,
   "Sic temper!" 'tis the proud refrain
   That baffles minions back amain,
   Maryland, my Maryland!
   Arise in majesty again,   ⎤ sung to last 4 bars
   Maryland, my Maryland!   ⎦

51

6. Come! for thy shield is bright and strong,
   Maryland, my Maryland!
   Come! for thy dalliance does thee wrong,
   Maryland, my Maryland!
   Come to thine own heroic throng
   Stalking with liberty along,
   And chant thy dauntless slogan-song,
   Maryland, my Maryland!

7. I see the blush upon thy cheek,
   Maryland, my Maryland!
   But thou wast ever bravely meek,
   Maryland, my Maryland!
   But lo! there surges forth a shriek,
   From hill to hill, from creek to creek,
   Potomac calls to Chesapeake,
   Maryland, my Maryland!

8. Thou wilt not yield the vandal toll,
   Maryland, my Maryland!
   Thou wilt not crook to his control,
   Maryland, my Maryland!
   Better the fire upon thee roll,
   Better the shot, the blade, the bowl,
   Than crucifixion of the soul,
   Maryland, my Maryland!

9. I hear the distant thunder-hum,
   Maryland, my Maryland!
   The "Old Line's" bugle, fife, and drum,
   Maryland, my Maryland!
   She is not dead, nor deaf, nor dumb;
   Huzza! she spurns the northern scum —
   She breathes! She burns! She'll come! She'll come!
   Maryland, my Maryland!

The Young Volunteer

John Hill Hewitt was born in New York in 1801, but settled in the South in 1823. He was a prolific composer of songs which championed the cause of the Confederacy.

Words and music by John Hill Hewitt

March ♩ = 120

young_____ vol – un – teer, and my heart is true To our

flag that woos the wind; Then three cheers_____ for that flag and our

coun – try too, And the girls we leave be – hind.

Chorus

Then a – dieu,_____ then a – dieu, 'tis the last_____ bu – gle's strain, That is

falling on the ear; Should it so____ be de-creed that we ne'er meet a-gain, Oh, re-mem-ber the Young Vol-un-teer.

2. When over the desert, through burning rays,
   With a heavy heart I tread;
   Or when I breast the cannon's blaze,
   And bemoan my comrades dead,
   Then, then I will think of my home and you,
   And our flag shall kiss the wind;
   With huzza for our cause and our country too,
   And the girls we leave behind. *Chorus*

We Conquer or Die

Although James Pierpont strove to rally the South with the apocalyptic theme of victory or death, he is remembered as the composer of a kinder and gentler song: "Jingle Bells."

Words and music by James Pierpont

The war drum is beat-ing, pre-pare for the fight, The stern big-ot North-man ex-ults___ in his might. Gird on your bright weap-ons your foe-men are nigh, And

this be our watch-word, "We con-quer or die!" And

this be our watch-word, "We con-quer or die!"

2. The trumpet is sounding from mountain to shore,
   Your swords and your lances must slumber no more,
   Fling forth to the sunlight your banner on high,
   Inscribed with the watchword: "We conquer or die!"
   Inscribed with the watchword: "We conquer or die!"

3. March on to the battlefield, there to do or dare,
   With shoulder to shoulder all danger to share,
   And let your proud watchword ring up to the sky,
   Till the blue arch re-echoes, "We conquer or die!"
   Till the blue arch re-echoes, "We conquer or die!"

4. Press forward undaunted, nor think of retreat,
   The enemy's host on the threshold to meet,
   Strike firm, till the foeman before you shall fly,
   Appalled by the watchword, "We conquer or die!"
   Appalled by the watchword, "We conquer or die!"

5. Go forth in the pathway our forefathers trod,
   We too fight for Freedom, our Captain is God,
   Their blood in our veins, with their honors we vie,
   Their's, too, was the watchword, "We conquer or die!"
   Their's, too, was the watchword, "We conquer or die!"

6. We strike for the South - Mountain, Valley, and Plain,
   For the South we will conquer, again and again;
   Her day of salvation and triumph is nigh,
   Our's then be the watchword, "We conquer or die!"
   Our's then be the watchword, "We conquer or die!"

Stonewall Jackson's Way

The Battle of Bull Run, July 21, 1861: "...Overwhelmed by superior numbers, and compelled to yield before a fire that swept everything before it, General Bee rode up and down his lines, encouraging his troops, by everything that was dear to them, to stand up and repel the tide that threatened them with destruction. At last his own brigade dwindled to a mere handful, with every field officer killed or disabled. He rode up to General Jackson and said, 'General, they are beating us back.'

"The reply was: 'Sir, we'll give them the bayonet.'

"General Bee immediately rallied the remnant of his brigade, and his last words to them were: 'There is Jackson standing like a stone wall. Let us determine to die here and we will conquer. Follow me!'" (*Charleston Mercury, July 25, 1861*)

Words by J. W. Palmer
Music: unknown

Come, stack arms, men,____ pile on the rails, Stir up the camp-fire bright;_____ No mat-ter if____ the can-teen fails, We'll make a roar-ing night._____ Here Shen-an-do-ah brawls a-long, Here

bur — ly Blue___ Ridge ech — oes strong, To swell the Bri — gade's
rous — ing song of Stone — wall Jack — son's way._____

2. We see him now-the old slouched hat
   Cocked o'er his eye askew.
   The shrewd, dry smile, the speech so pat,
   So calm, so blunt, so true;
   The "Blue Light Elder" knows 'em well:
   Says he, "That's Banks, he's fond of shell;
   Lord, save his soul! we'll give him"— well
   That's Stonewall Jackson's way.

3. Silence! Ground arms! Kneel all! Caps off!
   Old "Blue Light's" going to pray;
   Strangle the fool that dares to scoff!
   Attention! It's his way!
   Appealing from his native sod,
   "Hear us, Almighty God!
   Lay bare Thine arm, stretch forth Thy rod,
   Amen!" That's Stonewall Jackson's way.

4. He's in the saddle now! Fall in !
   Steady! The whole brigade!
   Hill's at the ford, cut off-we'll win
   His way out, ball and blade!
   What matter if our shoes are worn?
   What matter if our feet are torn?
   "Quick-step! We're with him before dawn!"
   That's Stonewall Jackson's way.

5. The sun's bright lances rout the mists
   Of morning, and, by George!
   Here's Longstreet struggling in the lists,
   Hemmed in an ugly gorge.
   Pope and his Yankees, whipped before,
   "Bayonets and grape!" Hear Stonewall roar;
   "Charge, Stuart! Pay off Ashby's score!"
   Is Stonewall Jackson's way.

6. Ah, maiden, wait, and watch, and yearn
   For news of Stonewall's band!
   Ah, Widow, read, with eyes that burn,
   That ring upon thy hand!
   Ah, wife, sew on, pray on, hope on!
   Thy life shall not be all forlorn.
   The foe had better ne'er been born
   That gets in Stonewall's way.

Riding a Raid

General James Ewell Brown ("Jeb") Stuart was famed for his daring and brilliant cavalry raids behind, around, and into Union lines. On December 28, 1862, after capturing a telegraph station on the Orange and Alexandria Railroad at Burke Station in northern Virginia, he sent the following telegram to Lincoln, in which he "complained" about the inferior quality of the captured Union mules:

President Lincoln:

The last draw of wagons I've just made are very good, but the mules are inferior stock, scarcely able to haul off the empty wagons; and if you expect me to give your lines any further attention in this quarter, you should furnish better stock, as I've had to burn several valuable wagons before getting them in my lines.

(Signed) J. E. B. Stuart

Words: anonymous
Music: "Bonnie Dundee"

'Tis old Stone – wall, the Reb – el, that leans on his sword, And while we are mount–ing, prays low to the Lord: "Now each cav–a – lier that loves Hon – or and Right, Let him fol–low the feath–er of Stu–art to – night." Come

tight – en your girth   and   slack – en your rein;   Come buck – le your blan – ket and

hol – ster a – gain;   Try the   click   of your   trig – ger and

bal – ance your blade,   For___ he must ride sure that goes   Rid – ing a   Raid!

2. Now gallop, now gallop, to swim or to ford!
   Old Stonewall, still watching, prays low to the Lord:
   "Good-bye dear old Rebel! The river's not wide,
   And Maryland's lights in her window to guide." *Chorus*

3. There's a man in a white house with blood on his mouth!
   If there's Knaves in the North, there are braves in the South.
   We are three thousand horses, and not one afraid;
   We are three thousand sabres and not a dull blade. *Chorus*

4. Then gallop, then gallop, by ravines and rocks!
   Who would bar us the way take his toll in hard knocks;
   For with these points of steel, on the line of Penn,
   We have made some fine strokes - and we'll make 'em again.   *Chorus*

Southrons' Chaunt of Defiance

The words to this song are credited to "a Lady of Kentucky." A. E. Blackmar set these melodramatic lyrics to an equally flamboyant tune—complete with unexpected modulations. He then published the work in New Orleans in 1864.

by A. E. Blackmar

With determination ♩ = 92

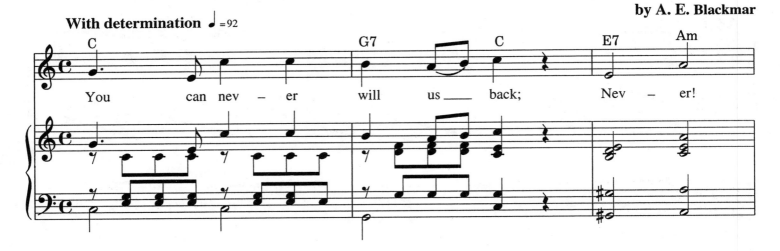

You can nev – er will us ___ back; Nev – er!

Nev – er! Tho' we per – ish in the track of

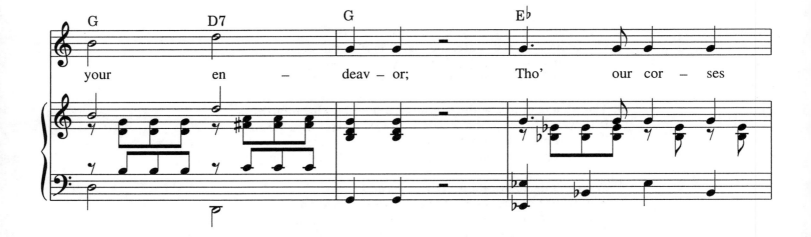

your en – deav – or; Tho' our cor – ses

strew the earth smil – ing now as on our birth,

And tho' blood pol – lute each _ hearth now _____ and _ ev – er.

2. We have risen to a man,
   Stern and fearless;
   Of your curses, of your ban,
   We are careless.
   Ev'ry hand is on its knife,
   Ev'ry gun is primed for strife.
   Ev'ry palm contains a Life
   High and peerless.

3. You have no such blood as ours
   For the shedding;
   In the veins of Cavaliers
   Was it heading!
   You have no such stately men
   In your abolition den
   Marching on through for and fen,
   Nothing dreading!

4. We may fall before the fire
   Of your legions,
   Paid with gold for murderous hire,
   Bought allegiance;
   But for every drop you shed,
   You shall have a mound of dead,
   So that vultures may be fed
   In our regions!

5. But the battle to the strong
   Is not given,
   While the Judge of right and wrong
   Sits in heaven.
   And the God of David still
   Guides the pebble with His will,
   There are giants yet to kill,
   Wrongs unshriven!

Lincoln

Old Abe Lincoln Came Out of the Wilderness

"Torchlight processions of Republicans sang this in the summer and fall months of 1860. The young Wide Awakes burbled it as the kerosene dripped on their blue oilcloth capes. Quartets and octettes jubilated with it in packed, smoky halls where audiences waited for speakers of the evening. In Springfield, Illinois, the Tall Man who was a candidate for the presidency of the nation, heard his two boys, Tad and Willie, sing it at him." (*Carl Sandburg,* **The American Songbag**)

Words: anonymous
Music: "Down in Alabam" (by J. Warner)

Old Abe Lin–coln came out of the wil – der-ness, out of the wil –der-ness, out of the wil – der-ness, Old Abe Lin–coln came out of the wil – der-ness, Man–y long years a – go.

Chorus

Man—y long years a — go, man—y long years a — go,

Old Abe Lin-coln came out of the wil—der-ness, man-y long years a — go.

2. Old Jeff Davis tore down the government,
tore down the government,
tore down the government,
Old Jeff Davis tore down the government,
Many long years ago. *Chorus*

3. But old Abe Lincoln built up a better one,
built up a better one,
built up a better one,
Old Abe Lincoln built up a better one,
Many long years ago. *Chorus*

Lincoln And Liberty

This wonderful Irish tune, "Old Rosin, the Beau," has had numerous American reincarnations. It surfaced as a campaign song for William Henry Harrison in the presidential election campaign of 1840 as "Old Tippecanoe." In 1844, as "Two Dollars a Day and Roast Beef," it helped James K. Polk defeat Henry Clay. In 1888 it worked for Benjamin Harrison against Grover Cleveland ("Tippecanoe and Morton Too"); but, in an 1892 rewrite ("Grandfather's Hat," still trading on the memory of his grandfather, Old Tippecanoe, William Henry Harrison) it backfired—Cleveland won.

Somewhere along the line it traveled out West, where as "The Old Settler's Song" it complained about the difficulties of prospecting and farming, and extolled the joys of being surrounded by "acres of clams" in Puget Sound. What we have here is its 1860 version, composed by the Abolitionist singer Jesse Hutchinson.

Words by Jesse Hutchinson
Music: "Old Rosin, the Beau"

68

2. They'll find what by felling and mauling,
   Our railmaker statesman can do;
   For the people are everywhere calling
   For Lincoln and Liberty too.
   Then up with the banner so glorious,
   The star-spangled red, white, and blue,
   We'll fight till our banner's victorious,
   For Lincoln and Liberty, too.

3. Our David's good sling is unerring,
   The Slavocrat's giant he slew,
   Then shout for the freedom preferring,
   For Lincoln and Liberty, too.
   We'll go for the son of Kentucky,
   The hero of Hoosierdom through,
   The pride of the "Suckers" so lucky,
   For Lincoln and Liberty, too.

The Liberty Ball

Words by Jesse Hutchinson
Music: "Old Rosin, the Beau"

1. Come all ye true friends of the nation,
   Attend to humanity's call;
   Come aid in the slave's liberation,
   And roll on the Liberty Ball.

   And roll on the Liberty Ball,
   And roll on the Liberty Ball,
   Come aid in the slave's liberation,
   And roll on the Liberty Ball.

2. We're foes unto wrong and oppression,
   No matter which side of the sea,
   And ever intend to oppose them
   Till all of God's image are free.

   Till all of God's image are free,
   Till all of God's image are free,
   And ever intend to oppose them,
   Till all of God's image are free.

3. We'll finish the temple of freedom,
   And make it capacious within,
   That all who seek shelter may find it
   Whatever the hue of their skin.

   Whatever the hue of their skin,
   Whatever the hue of their skin,
   That all who seek shelter may find it,
   Whatever the hue of their skin.

4. Success to the old-fashioned doctrine,
   That men are created all free;
   And down with the power of the despot,
   Wherever his strongholds may be.

   Wherever his strongholds may be,
   Wherever his strongholds may be,
   And down with the power of the despot,
   Wherever his strongholds may be.

5. The liberty hosts are advancing,
   For freedom to all, they declare,
   The downtrodden millions are sighing,
   Come break up our gloom of despair.

   Come break up our gloom of despair,
   Come break up our gloom of despair,
   The downtrodden millions are sighing,
   Come break up our gloom of despair.

(Repeat first verse)

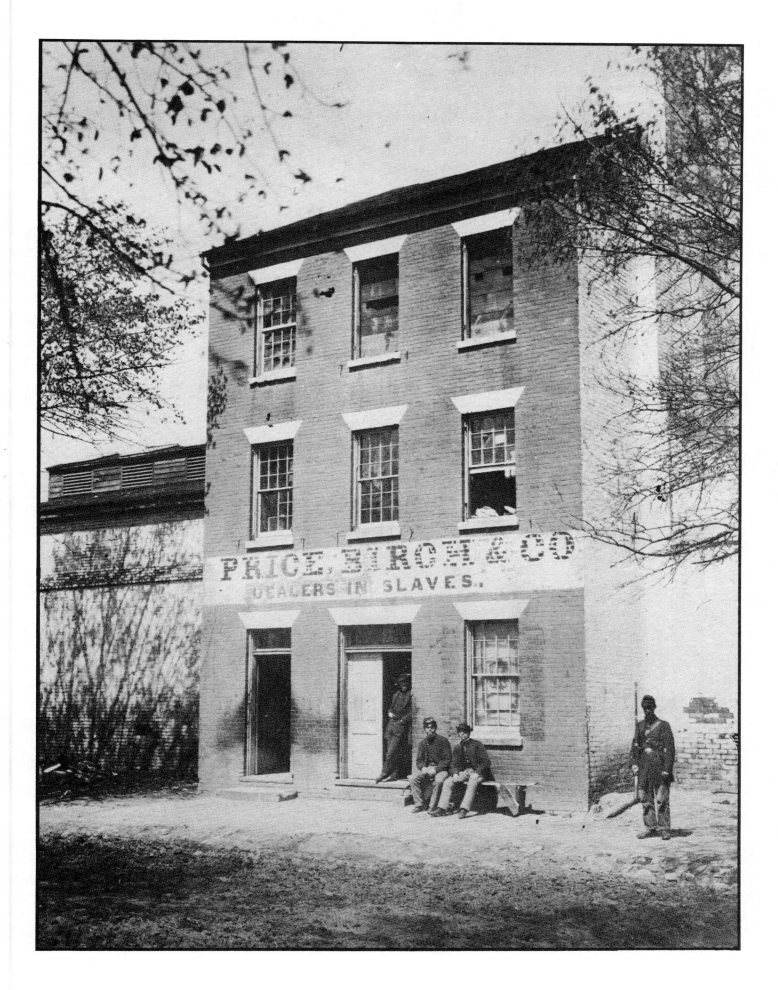

Abraham's Daughter

The "Fire Zou-Zous" (Fire Zouaves) were Union soldiers outfitted *à la Zouave*—that is, in the extravagant and highly colorful manner of the Zouave Corps in the French army. Like most Northerners of the time, composer Septimus Winner was captivated by the Zouaves' white turbans, blue shirts, and red pantaloons. He was a prolific song writer. One of Winner's winners is "Listen to the Mockingbird," written under the *nom de plume* of Alice Hawthorne (!).

Words and music by Septimus Winner

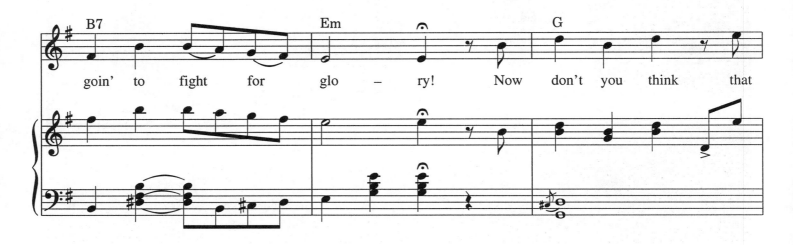

2. Oh! should you ask me who she am,
   Columbia is her name, sir;
   She is the child of Abraham,
   Or Uncle Sam, the same, sir.
   Now if I fight, why ain't I right?
   And don't you think I oughter.
   The volunteers are a-pouring in
   From every loyal quarter,
   And I'm goin' down to Washington
   To fight for Abraham's Daughter.

3. They say we have no officers,
   But ah! they are mistaken;
   And soon you'll see the Rebels run,
   With all the fuss they're makin';
   For there is one who just sprung up,
   He'll show the foe no quarter,
   (McClellan is the man I mean)
   You know he hadn't oughter,
   For he's gone down to Washington
   To fight for Abraham's Daughter.

73

4. We'll have a spree with Johnny Bull,
   Perhaps some day or other,
   And won't he have his fingers full,
   If not a deal of bother;
   For Yankee boys are just the lads
   Upon the land or water;
   And won't we have a "bully" fight,
   And don't you think we oughter,
   If he is caught at any time
   Insulting Abraham's Daughter.

5. But let us lay all jokes aside,
   It is sorry question;
   The man who would these states divide
   Should hang for his suggestion.
   One Country and one Flag, I say,
   Whoe'er the war may slaughter;
   So I'm goin' as a Fire Zou-Zou,
   And don't you think I oughter,
   I'm goin' down to Washington
   To fight for Abraham's Daughter.

Abraham's Daughter, II

Chorus

if they call up–on___ this___ child, I'ze bound to die a___ mar – tyr. For___

I be – long to the Fire Zou–Zous, And___ don't you think I ought – er? I'm___

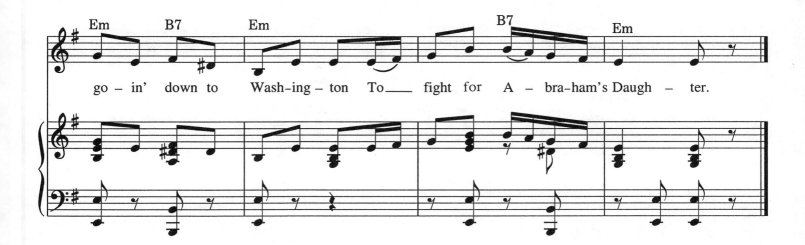

go – in' down to Wash–ing – ton To___ fight for A – bra–ham's Daugh – ter.

2. I am tired of a city life,
   And I will join the Zou-Zous;
   I'm going to try and make a hit
   Down among the Southern foo-foos;
   But if perchance I should get hit,
   I'll show them I'm a tartar;
   We are bound to save our Union yet,
   'Tis all that we are arter. *Chorus*

3. There is one thing more that I would state,
   Before I close my ditty,
   'Tis all about the volunteers
   That's left our good old city.
   They have gone to fight for the Stars and Stripes
   Our Union, now or never!
   We will give three cheers for the volunteers,
   And Washington forever. *Chorus*

We Are Coming, Father Abr'am

Although the response to Lincoln's July 1862 call for 300,000 volunteers was painfully slow, Quaker James Sloan Gibbons quickly came forward with this poem which was set to music with equal rapidity by several composers, including this version by Luther O. Emerson. With the inducement of bounty payments for enlistees (partially payable in advance of honorable discharge), the quota was surpassed before the end of 1862; some 421,000 men had enlisted for three years.

Words by James Sloan Gibbons
Music by L. O. Emerson

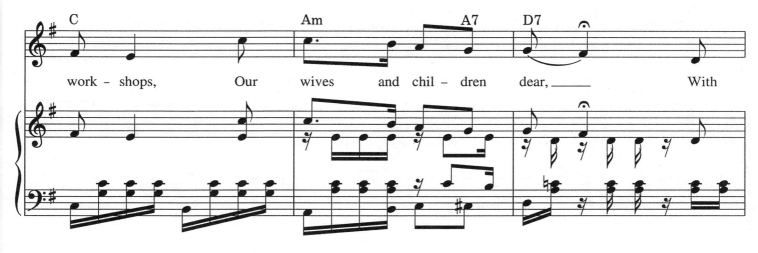

work - shops, Our wives and chil - dren dear, _____ With

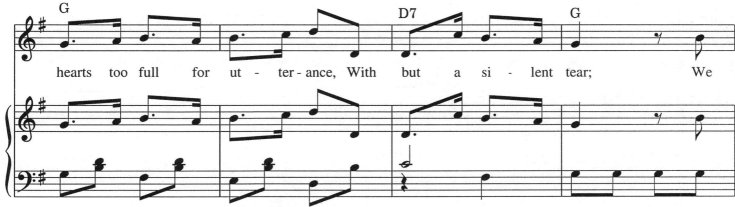

hearts too full for ut - ter - ance, With but a si - lent tear; We

dare not look be - hind us, But stead - fast - ly be - fore. We are

com - ing, Fa - ther A - br'am, Three hun - dred thou - sand more!

Chorus

We are com-ing, we are com-ing, Our Un-ion to re-

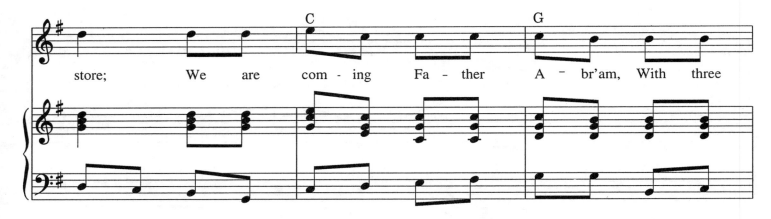

store; We are com-ing Fa-ther A-br'am, With three

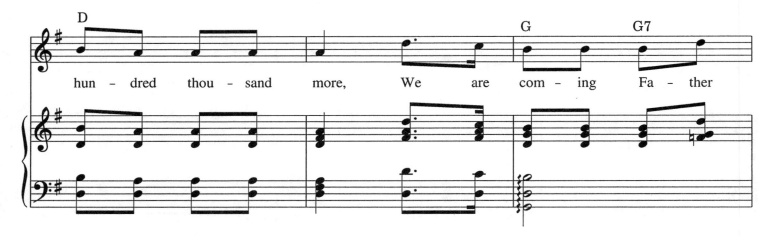

hun-dred thou-sand more, We are com-ing Fa-ther

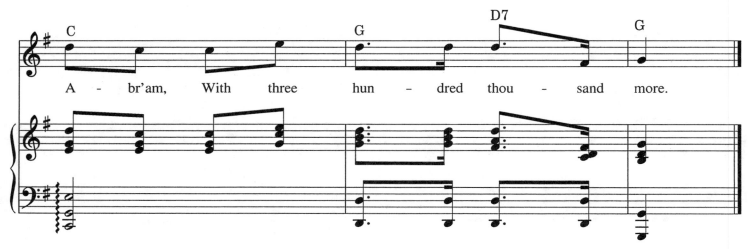

A-br'am, With three hun-dred thou-sand more.

2. If you look across the hilltops
   That meet the northern sky,
   Long moving lines of rising dust
   Your vision may descry;
   And now the wind, an instant,
   Tears the cloudy veil aside,
   And floats aloft our spangled flag
   In glory and in pride;
   And bayonets in the sunlight gleam,
   And bands brave music pour.
   We are coming, Father Abr'am,
   Three hundred thousand more!   *Chorus*

3. If you look all up our valleys
   Where the growing harvests shine,
   You may see our sturdy farmer boys
   Fast forming into line;
   And children from their mother's knees
   Are pulling at the weeds,
   And learning how to reap and sow
   Against their country's needs;
   And a farewell group stands weeping
   At every cottage door.
   We are coming, Father Abr'am,
   Three hundred thousand more!   *Chorus*

4. You have called us and we're coming
   By Richmond's bloody tide,
   To lay us down for Freedom's sake,
   Our brothers' bones beside;
   Or from foul treason's savage group,
   To wrench the murderous blade;
   And in the face of foreign foes
   Its fragments to parade;
   Six hundred thousand loyal men
   And true have gone before.
   We are coming, Father Abr'am,
   Three hundred thousand more!   *Chorus*

We'll Fight for Uncle Abe

Words by C. E. Pratt
Music by Frederick Buckley

Way down in old Var - gin - ni, I sup - pose you all do know, They have

tried to bust the Un - ion, But they find it is no go; The

Yan - kee boys are start – ing out The Un – ion for to save, And we're

go – ing down to Wash – ing -ton To fight for Un – cle Abe.

Chorus

Rip, Rap, Flip, Flap, Strap your knap - sack on your back, For

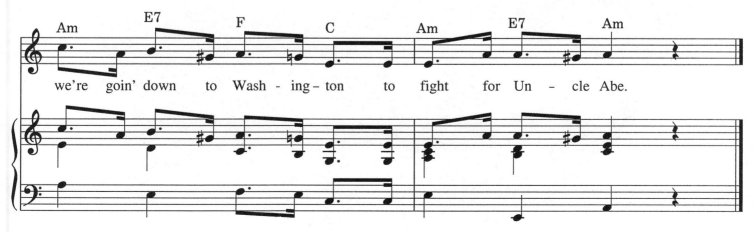

we're goin' down to Wash – ing -ton to fight for Un – cle Abe.

81

2. There is General Grant at Vicksburg,
   Just see what he has done,
   He has taken sixty cannon
   And made the Rebels run,
   And next he will take Richmond,
   I'll bet you half a dollar,
   And if he catches General Johnson,
   Oh won't he make him holler.   *Chorus*

3. The season now is coming
   When the roads begin dry;
   Soon the Army of the Potomac
   Will make the Rebels fly,
   For General McClellan, he's the man,
   The Union for to save;
   Oh! Hail Columbia's right side up,
   And so's your Uncle Abe.   *Chorus*

4. You may talk of Southern chivalry
   And cotton being king,
   But I guess before the war is done
   You'll think another thing;
   They say that recognition
   Will the Rebel country save,
   But Johnny Bull and Mister France
   Are 'fraid of Uncle Abe.   *Chorus*

82

Booth Killed Lincoln

"Through the general hum...came the muffled sound of a pistol shot...and then...a man ...leaps to the stage below.... Booth, the murderer...launches out in a firm and steady voice the words *Sic semper tyrannis*—and then walks...across the stage and disappears....

"A moment's hush—a scream—the cry of *murder*—Mrs. Lincoln leaning out of the box, with ashy cheeks, with involuntary cry, pointing to the retreating figure, *He has kill'd the President.*" (*Walt Whitman, 1879*)

Ad lib.

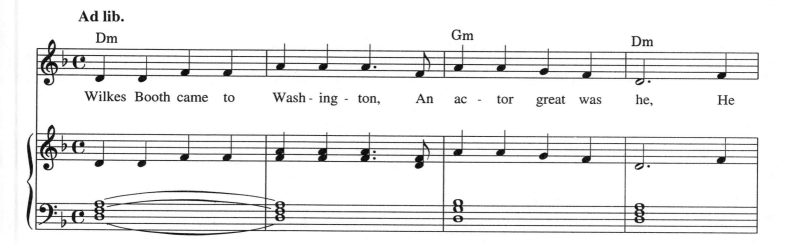

Wilkes Booth came to Wash-ing-ton, An ac - tor great was he, He

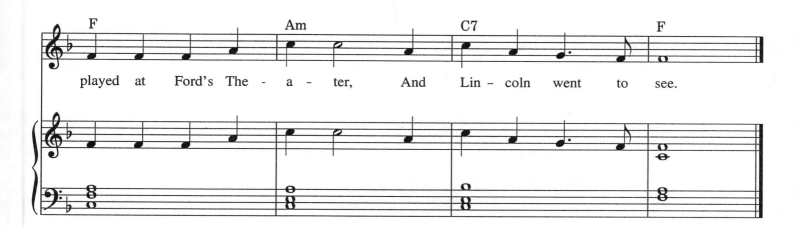

played at Ford's The - a - ter, And Lin - coln went to see.

2. It was early in April,
   Not many weeks ago,
   The people of this fair city
   All gathered at the show.

3. The war it is all over,
   The people happy now,
   And Abraham Lincoln
   Arose to make his bow;

4. The people cheer him wildly,
   Arising to their feet,
   And Lincoln waving of his hand,
   He calmly takes his seat.

5. And while he sees the play go on,
   His thoughts are running deep,
   His darling wife, close by his side,
   Has fallen fast asleep.

6. From the box there hangs a flag,
   It is not the Stars and Bars,
   The flag that holds within its folds
   Bright gleaming Stripes and Stars.

7. J. Wilkes Booth he move down the aisle,
   He had measured once before,
   He passes Lincoln's bodyguard
   A-nodding at the door.

8. He holds a dagger in his right hand,
   A pistol in his left,
   He shoots poor Lincoln in the temple,
   And sends his soul to rest.

9. The wife awakes from slumber,
   And screams in her rage,
   Booth jumps over the railing
   And lands him on the stage.

10. He'll rue the day, he'll rue the hour,
    As God him life shall give,
    When Booth stood in the center of the stage,
    Crying, "Tyrants shall not live!"

11. The people all excited then,
    Cried everyone, "A hand!"
    Cried all the people near,
    "For God's sake, save that man!"

12. Then Booth ran back with boot and spur
    Across the backstage floor,
    He mounts that trusty claybank mare,
    All saddled at the door.

13. J. Wilkes Booth, in his last play,
    All dressed in broadcloth deep,
    He gallops down the alleyway,
    I hear those horse's feet.

14. Poor Lincoln then was heard to say,
    And all has gone to rest,
    "Of all the actors in this town,
    I loved Wilkes Booth the best."

Universal Sentiments

In that great conflagration which all but consumed the nation, and out of which a stronger Union was forged, the feelings of the simple soldier far from home became an overriding symbol for both sides, which songwriters from the North and South could address in similar terms. While many of these plaints may strike our ears as lachrymose extravaganzas, the fact is that they expressed the way people really felt about the things that mattered. A struggle in which some 600,000 Americans were killed struck deeply into the lives of practically every family. Parting, dying in battle, those left behind—these universal themes were grist for the songwriters' mills. As contrasted with the rousing, patriotic songs that flowed from the composers' pens, these are the *lieder* of the period.

Unlike the political songs and the battle songs, these melancholy, often tragic ballads do not—need not—refer to specific incidents. It is not even necessary to know whether a song is either "Southern" or "Northern" to imagine how the emotions expressed touched both singer and listener alike.

That the professional songwriters of the period knew a good thing when they saw (heard) it, and sometimes tended to repeat themselves or attempted to imitate a "hit" song (for, indeed, many of these songs were hits), should not in any way trivialize these works which speak in the language of their time.

Weeping Sad and Lonely
(When This Cruel War Is Over)

Words by Charles C. Sawyer
Music by Henry Tucker

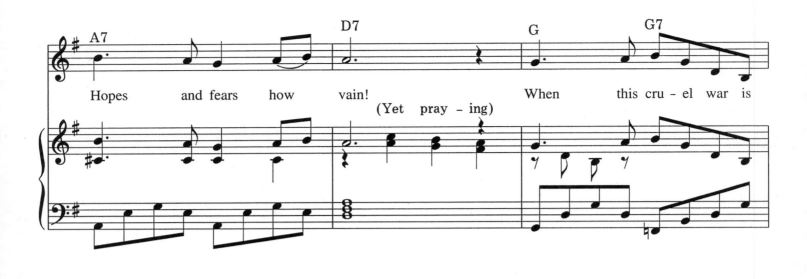

Hopes and fears how vain! When this cru - el war is
(Yet pray - ing)

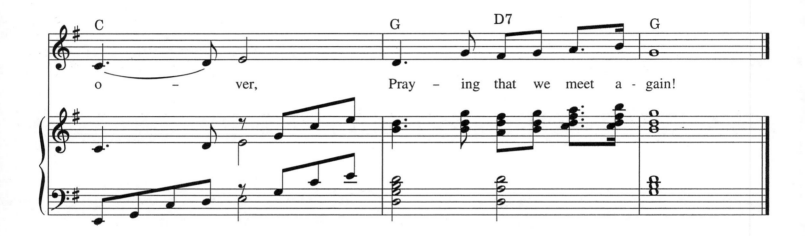

o - ver, Pray - ing that we meet a - gain!

2. When the summer breeze is sighing
   Mournfully along;
   Or when autumn leaves are falling,
   Sadly breathes the song.
   Oft in dreams I see thee lying
   On the battle plain,
   Lonely, wounded, even dying,
   Calling but in vain. *Chorus*

3. If amid the din of battle,
   Nobly you should fall,
   Far away from those who love you,
   None to hear you call,
   Who would whisper words of comfort,
   Who would soothe your pain?
   Ah! the many cruel fancies
   Ever in my brain. *Chorus*

4. But our country called you, darling,
   Angels cheer your way;
   While our nation's sons are fighting,
   We can only pray.
   Nobly strike for God and liberty,
   Let all nations see,
   How we love the starry banner,
   Emblem of the free. *Chorus*

Who Will Care for Mother Now?

Words and music by Charles C. Sawyer

com-rades, is this death? _____ Ah! how well I know your

an — swer; To my fate I meek – ly

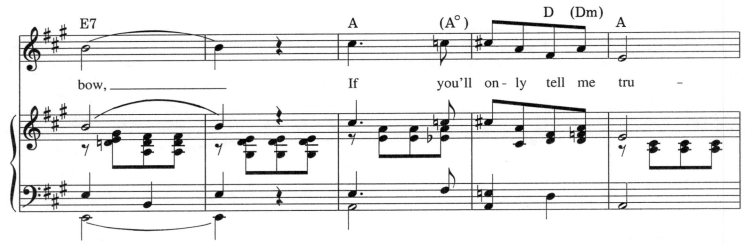

bow, _____ If you'll on - ly tell me tru –

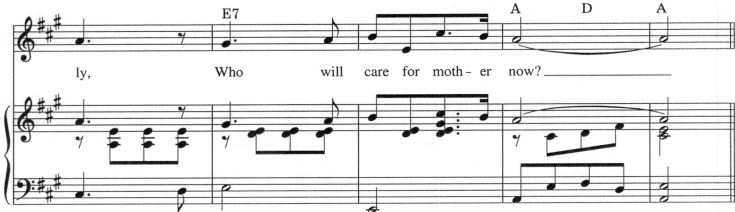

ly, Who will care for moth – er now? _____

90

Soon with an-gels I'll be march – ing, With bright lau-rels on my

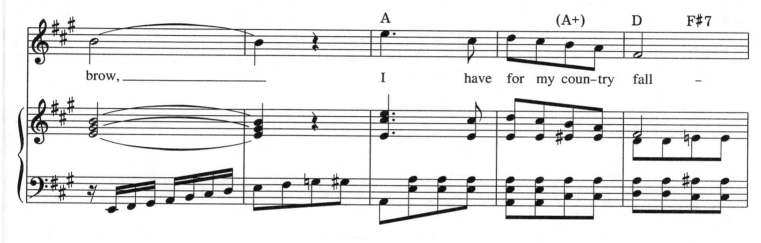

brow, _____ I have for my coun-try fall –

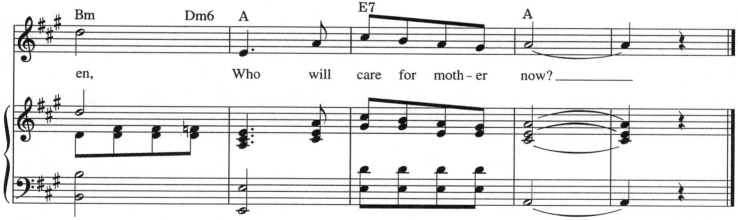

en, Who will care for moth – er now? _____

2. Who will comfort her in sorrow?
   Who will dry the falling tear?
   Gently smooth her wrinkled forehead?
   Who will whisper words of cheer?
   Even now I think I see her
   Kneeling, praying for me! How
   Can I leave her in anguish?
   Who will care for mother now?   *Chorus*

3. Let this knapsack be my pillow,
   And my mantle be the sky;
   Hasten, comrades, to the battle,
   I will like a soldier die.
   Soon with angels I'll be marching,
   With bright laurels on my brow;
   I have for my country fallen,
   Who will care for mother now?   *Chorus*

All Quiet Along the Potomac

(The Picket Guard)

Words by Mrs. Ethel Lynn Beers
Music by W. H. Goodwin

2. All quiet along the Potomac tonight,
   Where the soldiers lie peacefully dreaming,
   Their tents in the rays of the clear autumn moon,
   O'er the light of the watch fires, are gleaming;
   A tremulous sign, as the gentle night wind,
   Through the forest leaves softly is creeping,
   While stars up above, with their glittering eyes,
   Keep guard for the army is sleeping.

3. There's only the sound of the lone sentry's tread,
   As he tramps from the rock to the fountain,
   And thinks of the two in the low trundle bed,
   Far away in the cot on the mountain.
   His musket falls slack, and his face, dark and grim,
   Grows gentle with memories tender,
   As he mutters a prayer for the children asleep,
   For their mother, may Heaven defend her.

4. The moon seems to shine just as brightly as then,
   That night when the love yet unspoken
   Leaped up to his lips when low-murmured vows
   Were pledged to be ever unbroken.
   Then drawing his sleeve roughly over his eyes,
   He dashes off tears that are welling,
   And gathers his gun closer up to its place
   As if to keep down the heart-swelling.

5. He passes the fountain, the blasted pine tree,
   The footstep is lagging and weary;
   Yet onward he goes, through the broad belt of light,
   Toward the shades of the forest so dreary.
   Hark! Was it the night wind that rustled the leaves?
   Was it moonlight so wondrously flashing?
   It looks like a rifle — "Ah! Mary, good-bye!"
   And the lifeblood is ebbing and splashing.

6. All quiet along the Potomac tonight,
   No sound save the rush of the river;
   While soft falls the dew on the face of the dead—
   [*Skip to last beat of fourth from last measure*]
   The picket's off duty forever.

Do They Miss Me at Home?

Words by Caroline A. Mason
Music by S. M. Grannis

fire - side were think-ing of me as I roam, _____ Oh,

yes, 'twould be joy be-yond meas-ure, To know that they missed me at

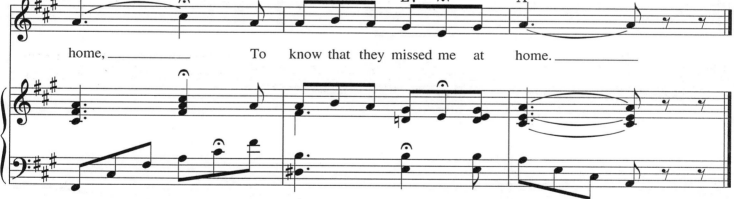

home, _____ To know that they missed me at home. _____

2. When twilight approaches, the season
That ever is sacred to song;
Does someone repeat my name over,
And sigh that I tarry so long?
And is there a chord in the music,
That's missed when my voice is away,
And a chord in each heart that awaketh
Regret at my wearisome stay?
Regret at my wearisome stay?

3. Do they set me a chair near the table
When evening's home pleasures are nigh,
When the candles are lit in the parlor,
And the stars in the calm azure sky?
And when the "good nights" are repeated,
And all lay them down to their sleep,
Do they think of the absent, and waft me
A whispered "good night" while they weep?
A whispered "good night" while they weep?

4. Do they miss me at home – do they miss me,
At morning, at noon, or at night?
And lingers one gloomy shade round them
That only my presence can light?
Are joys less invitingly welcome,
And pleasures less hale than before,
Because one is missed from the circle,
Because I am with them no more?
Because I am with them no more?

Lorena

Words by Rev. H. D. L. Webster
Music by J. P. Webster

The years creep slow-ly by, Lo-

re - na, The snow is on the grass a - gain; The

sun's low down the sky, Lo - re - na, The frost gleams where the flow'rs have

2. A hundred months have passed, Lorena,
   Since last I held that hand in mine,
   And felt the pulse beat fast, Lorena,
   Though mine beat faster far than tine.
   A hundred months, 'twas flowery May,
   When up the hilly slope we climbed,
   To watch the dying of the day,
   And hear the distant church bells chime.

3. We loved each other then, Lorena,
   More than we ever dared to tell;
   And what we might have been, Lorena,
   Had but our lovings prospered well –
   But then, 'tis past, the years are gone,
   I'll not call up their shadowy forms;
   I'll say to them, "Lost years, sleep on!
   Sleep on! nor heed life's pelting storms."

4. The story of that past, Lorena,
   Alas! I care not to repeat,
   The hopes that could not last,
     Lorena,
   They lived, but only lived to cheat.
   I would not cause e'en one regret
   To rankle in your bosom now;
   For "if we *try,* we may forget,"
   Were words of thine long years ago.

5. Yes, these were words of thine,
     Lorena,
   They burn within my memory yet;
   They touched some tender chords,
     Lorena,
   Which thrill and tremble with
     regret.

   'Twas not thy woman's heart that
     spoke;
   Thy heart was always true to me:
   A duty, stern and pressing broke
   The tie which linked my soul
     with thee.

6. It matters little now, Lorena,
   The past is in the eternal past;
   Our heads will soon lie low, Lorena,
   Life's tide is ebbing out so fast.
   There is a Future! O, thank God!
   Of life this is so small a part!
   'Tis dust to dust beneath the sod;
   But there, *up there,* 'tis heart to
     heart.

The Vacant Chair

(We Shall Meet but We Shall Miss Him)

Words by Henry S. Washburn
Music by George F. Root

Poignantly ♩ = 69

We shall meet but we shall miss him, There will be one va-cant

chair; We shall lin - ger to ca - ress him, While we

breathe our ev - 'ning pray'r; When a year a - go we

gath - ered, Joy was in his mild blue eye, But a

gold — en chord is sev-ered, And our hopes in ru-in lie. We shall

Chorus

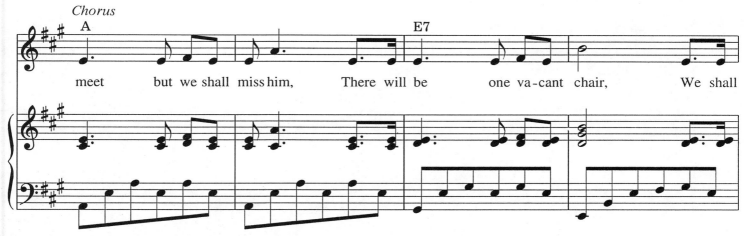

meet but we shall miss him, There will be one va-cant chair, We shall

lin - ger to ca-ress him When we breathe our ev-'ning pray'r.

2. At our fireside, sad and lonely,
   Often will the bosom swell
   At remembrance of the story,
   How our noble Willie fell;
   How he strove to bear our banner
   Through the thickest of the fight,
   And uphold our country's honor,
   In the strength of manhood's night. *Chorus*

3. True, they tell us wreaths of glory
   Ever more will deck his brow,
   But this soothes the anguish only,
   Sweeping o'er our heartstrings now.
   Sleep today, oh early fallen,
   In thy green and narrow bed,
   Dirges from the pine and cypress
   Mingle with the tears we shed. *Chorus*

Home, Sweet Home

Words by John Howard Payne
Music by Henry Rowley Bishop

An exile from home, splendor dazzles in vain,
Oh, give me my lowly thatched cottage again;
The birds singing gaily, that come at my call;
Give me them, with that peace of mind, dearer than all.

Chorus

2. To thee, I'll return, overburdened with care,
The heart's dearest solace will smile on me there.
No more from that cottage again will I roam,
Be it ever so humble, there's no place like home.

Chorus

The Drummer Boy of Shiloh

Words and music by Will S. Hays

day.   A wound-ed sol – dier held him up,   His drum was by his

side.   He clasped his hands,__ then__ raised his eyes,   And

prayed be - fore he died,_____ He clasped his hands, then raised his

eyes,   And prayed be - fore he died.

2. Look down upon the battle field,
   Oh, Thou our Heavenly Friend!
   Have mercy on our sinful souls!
   The soldiers cried, "Amen!"
   For gathered 'round a little group,
   Each brave man knelt and cried.
   They listened to the drummer boy
   Who prayed before he died.
   They listened to the drummer boy
   Who prayed before he died.

3. "Oh, mother," said the dying boy,
   "Look down from Heaven on me,
   Receive me to thy fond embrace –
   Oh, take me home to thee.
   I've loved my country as my God;
   To serve them both I've tried."
   He smiled, shook hands – death seized the boy
   Who prayed before he died.
   He smiled, shook hands –death seized the boy
   Who prayed before he died.

4. Each soldier wept, then, like a child –
   Stout hearts were they, and brave;
   The flag his winding sheet – God's Book
   The key unto his grave.
   They wrote upon a simple board
   These words: "This is a guide
   To those who'd mourn the drummer boy
   Who prayed before he died.
   To those who'd mourn the drummer boy
   Who prayed before he died.

5. Ye angels 'round the Throne of Grace,
   Look down upon the braves
   Who fought and died on Shiloh's plain,
   Now slumb'ring in their graves!
   How many homes made desolate –
   How many hearts have sighed –
   How many, like that drummer boy,
   Who prayed before they died;
   How many, like that drummer boy,
   Who prayed before they died!

The Southern Soldier Boy

Words by Captain G. W. Alexander
Music: "The Boy with the Auburn Hair"

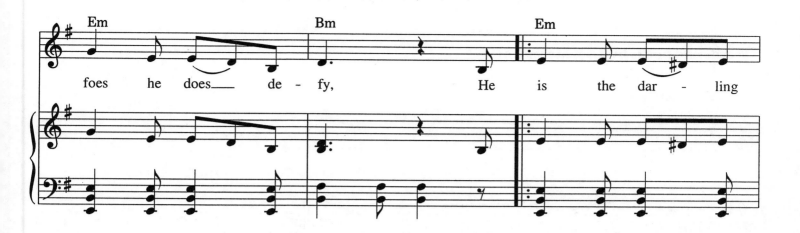

foes he does___ de - fy, He is the dar - ling

of my heart, My South - ern Sol - dier Boy. He Boy.

2. When Bob comes home from war's alarms,
   We'll start anew in life,
   I'll give myself right up to him,
   A dutiful, loving wife.
   I'll try my best to please my dear,
   For he is my only joy;
   He is the darling of my heart,
   My Southern Soldier Boy.
   He is the darling of my heart,
   My Southern Soldier Boy.

3. Oh! if in battle he was slain,
   I am sure that I should die;
   But I am sure he'll come again
   And cheer my weeping eye;
   But should he fall in this our glorious cause,
   He still would be my joy,
   For many a sweetheart mourns the loss
   Of a Southern Soldier Boy.
   For many a sweetheart mourns the loss
   Of a Southern Soldier Boy.

4. I hope for the best, and so do all
   Whose hopes are in the field;
   I know that we shall win the day,
   For Southrons never yield.
   And when we think of those that are away,
   We'll look above for joy,
   And I'm mighty glad that my Bobby is
   A Southern Soldier Boy.
   He is the darling of my heart,
   My Southern Soldier Boy.

The Faded Coat of Blue

Words and music by J. H. McNaughton

My ___ brave lad he sleeps in his

fad – ed coat of blue, In a lone – ly grave un – known lies the

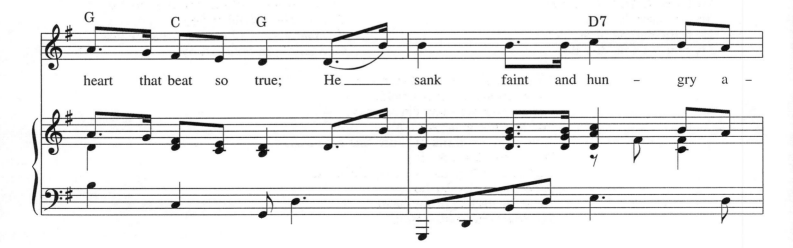

heart that beat so true; He ___ sank faint and hun – gry a –

mong the fam – ished brave, And they laid him sad and lone – ly with –

in his name-less grave.

Chorus

No more the bu – gle calls the wea – ry one,

Rest no – ble spir – it, in thy grave un-known! I'll __ find you and know you a –

mong the good and true, When a robe of white is giv'n for the fad – ed coat of blue.

2. He cried, "Give me water and just a little crumb,
   And my mother she will bless you through all the years
      to come;
   Oh! tell my sweet sister, so gentle, good and true,
   That I'll meet her up in heav'n in my faded coat of blue."
   Chorus

3. He said, "My dear comrades, you cannot take me home,
   But you'll mark my grave for mother, she'll find me if
      she'll come;
   I fear she'll not know me, among the good and true,
   When I meet her up in heav'n in my faded coat of blue."
   Chorus

4. Long, long years have vanished, and though he comes
      no more,
   Yet my heart with startling beats with each footfall at
      my door;
   I gaze o'er the hill where he waved a last adieu,
   But no gallant lad I see in his faded coat of blue. *Chorus*

5. No sweet voice was there, breathing soft a mother's prayer,
   But there's One who takes the brave and the true in
      tender care.
   No stone marks the sod o'er my lad so brave and true,
   In his lonely grave he sleeps in his faded coat of blue.
   Chorus

Somebody's Darling

Words by Marie Ravenal de la Coste
Music by John Hill Hewitt

In - to the ward of the clean white – washed halls,

Where the dead slept and the dy – ing lay; Wound- ed by bay- o - nets,

sa - bres and balls, Some-bod - y's dar - ling was borne one day.

2. Matted and damp are his tresses of gold,
   Kissing the snow of that fair young brow;
   Pale are the lips of most delicate mould,
   Somebody's darling is dying now.
   Back from his beautiful purple-veined brow,
   Brush off the wandering waves of gold;
   Cross his white hands on his broad bosom now,
   Somebody's darling is still and cold. *Chorus*

3. Give him a kiss, but for Somebody's sake,
   Murmur a prayer for him, soft and low;
   One little curl from his golden mates take,
   Somebody's pride they were once, you know;
   Somebody's warm hand has oft rested there,
   Was it a mother's so soft and white?
   Or have the lips of a sister, so fair,
   Ever been bathed in their waves of light? *Chorus*

4. Somebody's watching and waiting for him,
   Yearning to hold him again to her breast;
   Yet, there he lies with his blue eyes so dim,
   And purple, child-like lips half apart.
   Tenderly bury the fair, unknown dead,
   Pausing to drop on his grave a tear;
   Carve on the wooden slab over his head,
   "Somebody's darling is slumbering here." *Chorus*

Just Before the Battle, Mother

Words and music by George F. Root

view.

Com - rades brave are 'round me ly - ing,

Filled with thoughts of home and God; For well they know that on the

mor - row, Some will sleep be - neath the sod.

Chorus

Fare - well, Moth-er, you may nev - er Press me to your breast a -

gain; But, Oh, you'll not for-get me, Moth-er,

If I'm num-bered with the slain. _____

2. Oh, I long to see you, Mother,
   And the loving ones at home,
   But I'll never leave our banner,
   Till in honor I can come.
   Tell the traitors all around you
   That their cruel words we know,
   In every battle kill our soldiers
   By the help they give the foe. *Chorus*

3. Hark! I hear the bugles sounding,
   'Tis the signal for the fight,
   Now, may God protect us, Mother,
   As He ever does the right.
   Hear the "Battle Cry of Freedom,"
   How it swells upon the air,
   Oh, yes, we'll rally 'round the standard,
   Or we'll perish nobly there. *Chorus*

Just After the Battle

Words and music by George F. Root

Man - y sleep to wak-en nev - er,

In this world of strife and death, And man - y more are faint-ly

call - ing, With their fee- ble dy - ing breath.

Chorus

Moth - er, dear, your boy is wound - ed, And the night is drear with pain, But

123

still   I feel that I shall see   you,   And   the dear old home a - gain.

2. Oh, the first great charge was fearful,
And a thousand brave men fell,
Still amid the dreadful carnage,
I was safe from shot and shell.
So amid the fatal shower,
I had nearly passed the day,
When here the dreaded "minnie" struck me,
And I sunk amid the fray. *Chorus*

3. Oh, the glorious cheer of triumph,
When the foeman turned and fled,
Leaving us the field of battle,
Strewn with dying and with dead.
Oh the torture and the anguish,
That I could not follow on,
But here amid my fallen comrades,
I must wait till morning's dawn. *Chorus*

Soldiers' Songs

Tenting on the Old Camp Ground

When Walter Kittredge received his draft notice in 1863, his response was to write this song. Perhaps he imagined himself far from home, on some lonely and devastated battlefield; but this was never to be. He was rejected for military service because of a childhood brush with rheumatic fever. His song, however, fared better. It was published by the Oliver Ditson Company in Boston, and it enjoyed an enormous success both during and after the war.

Words and music by Walter Kittredge

2. We've been tenting tonight on the old camp ground,
   Thinking of days gone by,
   Of the loved ones at home that gave us the hand,
   And the tear that said, "Goodbye!" *Chorus*

3. We are tired of war on the old camp ground,
   Many are dead and gone,
   Of the brave and true who've left their homes,
   Others been wounded long. *Chorus*

4. We've been fighting today on the old camp ground,
   Many are lying near;
   Some are dead and some are dying,
   Many are in tears.

Final Chorus:
   Many are the hearts that are weary tonight,
   Wishing for the war to cease;
   Many are the hearts that are looking for the right
   To see the dawn of peace.
     Dying tonight, dying tonight,
     Dying on the old camp ground.

I'll Be a Sergeant

This is the American cousin of the British Army marching song "I've Got a Sixpence."

drum, _____ When _____ peace shall call us back from the camp and biv–ou–ac, And the drum taps, "March – ing home."

2. She sha'nt be Cap'n, that must not happen,
   She sha'nt be Cap'n, but play the second fife;
   We can bear the colors best,
   She shall wear them on her breast,
   Salute us, and "dress," and in short be our wife. *Chorus*

3. Should I be Col'nel, gazetted in the Journal,
   Oh, should I be Colonel, to lead in the strife,
   For her sake, so pround I'd be,
   And let every Rebel see,
   How a man can fight for a flag and a wife!

Final Chorus:
   For, dear girls, we soldiers adore you;
   Make us brave through your love, we implore you!
   Then happy shall we be
   To bend the suppliant knee,
   When we come marching home.
   Marching home, marching home, marching home,
   Marching home to the roll of the drum.
   Then, freed from war's alarms,
   To you we'll yield our arms,
   When the drum taps, "Marching home!"

Goober Peas

" 'Kin you writ me a letter?' drawled a whining voice from a bed in one of the wards, a cold day in '62. The speaker was an up-country Georgian, one of the kind called 'Goubers' by the soldiers generally...." So begins an anecdote recounted in Phoebe Yates Pember's *A Southern Woman's Story,* published in 1879. "Goubers," or "goobers" were peanuts, a staple part of the Georgians' diet in the lean days of the war. The first published version of this song (1866) credits its authorship to "A. Pindar, Esq." and "P. Nutt, Esq."—simply two other words for "goober."

2. When a horseman passes, the soldiers have a rule,
   To cry out at their loudest, "Mister, here's your mule!"
   But another pleasure enchantinger than these,
   Is wearing out your grinders, eating goober peas! *Chorus*

3. Just before the battle the Gen'ral hears a row,
   He says, "The Yanks are coming, I hear their rifles now."
   He turns around in wonder, and what do you think he sees?
   The Georgia Militia – eating goober peas! *Chorus*

4. I think my song has lasted almost long enough,
   The subject's interesting, but rhymes are mighty rough,
   I wish this war was over, when free from rags and fleas,
   We'd kiss our wives and sweethearts and gobble goober peas! *Chorus*

The New York Volunteer

The 11th New York Volunteer Infantry (New York Fire Zouaves) was formed early in the war. In the spring of 1861 it was yet possible to think and sing of the conflict as a gallant adventure.

Words: anonymous
Music: "Lincolnshire Poacher"

'Twas in the days ___ of sev – en – ty – six, When Free – men young and old, ___ All fought for In – de – pen – dence then, Each he – ro brave ___ and bold! ___ 'Twas then the no – ble Stars and Stripes In tri – umph did ___ ap –

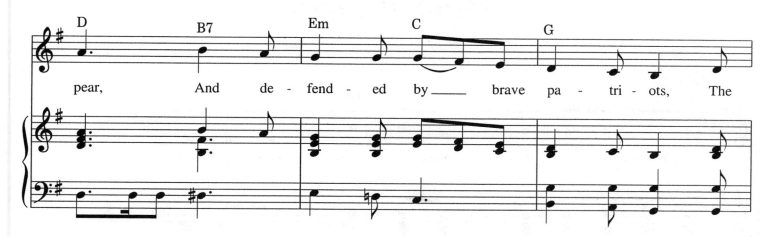

pear, And de - fend - ed by _____ brave pa - tri - ots, The

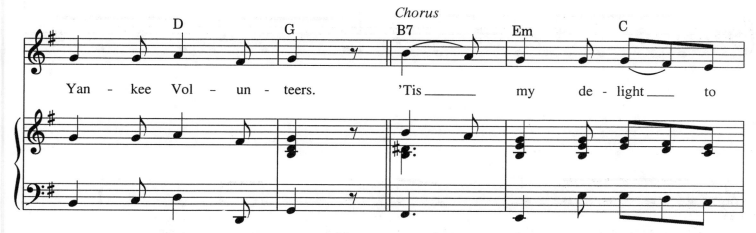

Chorus

Yan - kee Vol - un - teers. 'Tis _____ my de - light _____ to

march and fight Like a New York Vol - un - teer. _____ The

2. Now, there's our City Regiments,
   Just see what they have done:
   The first to offer to the State
   To go to Washington,
   To protect the Federal Capitol
   And the flag they love so dear!
   And they've done their duty nobly,
   Like New York Volunteers. *Chorus*

3. The Rebels out in Maryland,
   They madly raved and swore,
   They'd let none of our Union troops
   Pass through Baltimore;
   But the Massachusetts Regiment,
   No traitors did they fear;
   But fought their way to Washington,
   Like Yankee Volunteers. *Chorus*

Drink It Down

down,   drink it down,   drink it   down.

2. Here's success to Sherry,
   Drink it down, drink it down,
   Here's success to Sherry,
   Drink it down, drink it down.
   Here's success to Sherry,
   For it makes the heart beat merry,
   Drink it down, drink it down, drink it down.

3. Here's success to Whisky...
   For it makes the spirits frisky.

4. Here's success to Cider...
   For it makes the frame grow wider.

5. Here's success to Brandy...
   Just enough to make us handy.

6. Here's success to Ale...
   When it's made us strong and hale.

7. Here's success to Punch...
   With a little social lunch.

8. Here's success to Porter...
   While we use it as we oughter.

9. Here's success to Water...
   Heaven's draught that does no slaughter.

Farewell to Grog

On September 1, 1862, a law abolishing the grog (rum and water) ration in the Union Navy was enacted. The tradition of offering the tars their tot of rum had a long and honorable history, dating back to British naval tradition:

> Then each man took his tot of rum, and drunk success to trade,
> And likewise to the cabin boy who was neither man nor maid.
> Here's hoping the wars don't rise again, our sailors to destroy,
> And here's hoping for a jolly lot more like the handsome cabin boy.

Words by Caspar Schenk, U.S.N.
Music: "Landlord Fill the Flowing Bowl"

Come, mess- mates, pass the bot - tle 'round, Our
time is short, re - mem - ber, For our grog must stop, our
spir - its drop, On the first day of Sep - tem - ber.

Chorus

For to-night we'll mer-ry, mer-ry be, For to-night we'll mer-ry, mer-ry be,

For to-night we'll mer-ry, mer-ry be, To-mor-row we'll be so-ber.

2. Farewell old rye, 'tis a sad, sad word,
   But alas! It must be spoken,
   The ruby cup must be given up,
   And the demijohn be broken. *Chorus*

3. Jack's happy days will soon be gone,
   To return again, oh never!
   For they've raised his pay five cents a day,
   But stopped his grog forever. *Chorus*

4. Yet memory oft' will backward turn,
   And dwell with fondness partial,
   On the days when gin was not a sin,
   Nor cocktails brought court martial. *Chorus*

5. All hands to split the main brace, call,
   But split it now in sorrow,
   For the spirit-room key will be laid away
   Forever, on tomorrow. *Chorus*

The Old Union Wagon

The next two songs are parodies of "Wait for the Wagon," a pre–Civil War courting song. They provide yet another set of examples of how Northern and Southern lyricists seized upon a common musical tradition to express conflicting points of view.

Words by John Hogarth Lozier
Music: "Wait for the Wagon"

Now, in Un - cle Sam's Do - min - ion in eight - een six - ty one, Well the fight be - tween Se - ces - sion and Un - ion was be - gun. The south de - clared they'd

have the "rights" which Un – cle Sam de – nied, Or

in the se – cesh wag – on they'd all take a ride, Hur –

Chorus

rah for the wag – on The old Un – ion wag – on, We'll

stick to our wag – on, And we'll all take a ride.

2. The makers of our wagon were men of solid wit,
   They made it out of "Charter Oak" which would not rot or split.
   Its wheels are of material, the strongest and the best,
   And two are named the North and South, and two the East and West. *Chorus*

3. Our wagon bed is strong enough for any "revolution,"
   In fact it is the "hull" of the old *Constitution;*
   Her coupling's strong, her axle's long, and anywhere you get her,
   No Monarch's frown can "back her down"– no Traitor can upset her. *Chorus*

4. This good old Union Wagon, the nation all admired,
   Her wheels had run for four score years and never once been "tired,"
   Her passengers were happy as along her way she whirled,
   For the good old Union Wagon was the glory of the world. *Chorus*

The Southern Wagon

Words: anonymous
Music: "Wait for the Wagon"

1. Come all ye sons of freedom,
   And join our Southern band,
   We are going to fight the Yankees
   And drive them from our land.
   Justice is our motto,
   And Providence our guide,
   So jump into the wagon
   And we'll all take a ride.

Chorus
   So wait for the wagon!
   The dissolution wagon!
   The South is the wagon,
   And we'll all take a ride.

2. Secession is our watchword,
   Our rights we all demand;
   To defend our homes and firesides
   We pledge our hearts and hands;
   Jeff Davis is our President,
   With Stephens by his side;
   Brave Beauregard, our General,
   Will join us in the ride. *Chorus*

3. Our wagon is the very best,
   The running gear is good;
   Stuffed 'round the sides with cotton,
   And made of Southern wood.
   Carolina is the driver,
   With Georgia by her side,
   Virginia holds the flag up,
   And we'll all take a ride. *Chorus*

We've Drunk From the Same Canteen

"Private Miles O'Reilly" was in reality Charles Graham Halpine (1829–1868), who emigrated to America from Ireland before the Civil War. He worked for a while at the *Boston Post,* and subsequently moved to New York, where he worked for the *Herald,* the *Times,* and the *Tribune.* When the war broke out he joined the "Fighting Irish" New York 69th Regiment, where he rose from lieutenant to brigadier general.

By "Private Miles O'Reilly"

There are bonds of all sorts in this world of ours; Fet–ters of friend-ship and ties of flow-ers, And true lov–ers' knots, I ween._____ The boy and the girl are

bound by a kiss, But there's nev – er a bond,_ old friend, like this: We have

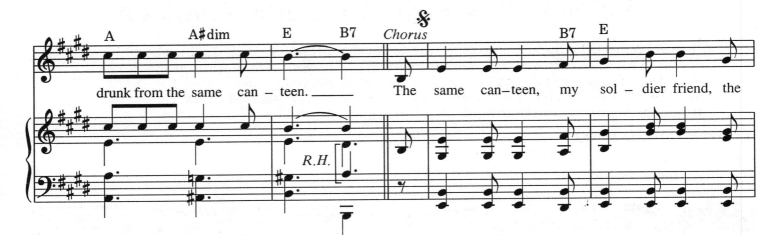

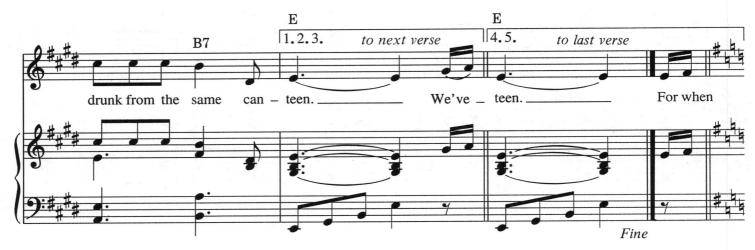

2. We've shared our blankets and tent together,
   And marched and fought in all kinds of weather,
   And hungry and full we've been.
   Had days of battle and days of rest,
   But this mem'ry I cling to and love the best;
   We have drunk from the same canteen. *Chorus*

3. The rich and the great sit down to dine,
   And they quaff to each other in sparkling wine,
   From glasses crystal and green.
   But I guess in their golden potations they miss
   The warmth of regard to be found in this;
   We have drunk from the same canteen. *Chorus*

4. It was sometimes water, and sometimes milk,
   And sometimes applejack fine as silk.
   But whatever the tipple has been,
   We shared it together in bane or bliss,
   And I warm to you, friend, when I think of this;
   We have drunk from the same canteen. *Chorus*

144

Slower-ad lib.

Last Verse

For when wound – ed I lay on the out – er slope, With my blood flow–ing fast, and but

lit – tle hope on which my faint spir – its might lean. _____ Oh,

a tempo

then, I re·mem·ber you crawled to my side, And bleed – ing so fast, it seemed

rit.

both must have died, We drunk from the same can – teen. _____ The

to Chorus

145

The Brass-Mounted Army

"The dislike of the private soldiers for quartermasters and commissaries was well-nigh universal.... The ragged jokers of our army never neglected an opportunity of making a hit at these officers.... The men used to call shot or shell that passed overhead and went far to the rear, 'Quartermaster hunters.' Upon one occasion, at Petersburg (June, 1864), during a severe artillery fire, a gallant fellow with more humor than prudence, jumped upon the parapet, and pointing to a shell then passing over, exclaimed: 'A little more to the right, a little more to the right, the quartermasters are *down behind that hill.*'" (**The Land We Love,** *September 1868*)

Oh, sol – diers I've con-clud – ed to
an – y be of-fend – ed at

make a lit – tle song, And if I tell no
what I have to sing, Then sure – ly his own

false – hood there can be noth – ing wrong; If
con – science ap – plies the bit – ter sting. Oh,

(to Chorus)

146

2. Whisky is a monster, and ruins great and small,
But in our noble army, Headquarters gets it all;
They drink it when there's danger, although it seems
too hard,
But if a private touches it they put him "under
guard." *Chorus*

3. And when we meet the ladies we're bound to go it sly,
Headquarters are the pudding, and the privates are
the pie!
They issue Standing Orders to keep us all in line,
For if *we* had a showing, the *brass* would fail to
shine. *Chorus*

4. At every big plantation or Negro-holder's yard,
Just to save the property, the general puts a guard;
The sentry's then instructed to let no private pass,
The rich man's house and table are fixed to suit the
"brass." *Chorus*

5. I have to change this story, so beautiful and true,
But the poor man and widow must have a line or two;
For them no guard is stationed, their fences oft are
burned,
And property molested, as long ago you've learned.
Chorus

6. The army's now much richer than when the war begun,
It furnishes three tables where once it had but one;
The first richly loaded with chickens, goose, and duck,
The rest with pork and mutton, the third with good
old buck. *Chorus*

7. Our generals eat the poultry, and buy it very cheap,
Our colonels and our majors devour the hog and sheep;
The privates are contented (except when they can
steal),
With beef and corn bread plenty to make a hearty
meal. *Chorus*

8. Sometimes we get so hungry that we're bound to
press a pig,
Then the largest stump in Dixie we're sure to have
to dig;
And when we fret, an officer who wears long-legged
boots,
With neither judge nor jury, puts us on "double
roots." *Chorus*

9. These things, and many others, are truly hard to me,
But still I'll be contented, and fight for Liberty!
And when the war is over, oh what a jolly time!
We'll be our own commanders and sing much
sweeter rhymes. *Chorus*

10. We'll see our loving sweethearts, and sometimes
kiss them too,
We'll eat the finest rations, and bid old buck adieu;
There'll be no generals with orders to compel,
Long boots and eagle buttons, forever fare ye well!

Final Chorus
And thus we'll leave the army, the brass-mounted
army,
The high-faluting army, where eagle buttons rule.

The Valiant Conscript

Colonel Zebulon Baird Vance, of the 26th North Carolina, although nominated for governor, continued to serve until his election in August 1862. On July 1, 1862, his brigade was involved in heavy fighting at Malvern Hill in defense of Richmond. At one point a terrified rabbit was seen racing across the field. Vance called out: "Run little cottontail! I'd run too if I wasn't governor of North Carolina!"

Music: "Yankee Doodle"

Chorus

Hold your head up, Shang-hai, Shanks, Don't shake your knees and blink ___ so, It is no time to dodge the act; Brave com-rades, don't you think so?

2. I was a ploughboy in the field,
   A gawky, lazy dodger,
   When came the conscript officer
   And took me for a sodger.
   He put a musket in my hand,
   And showed me how to fire it;
   I marched and counter-marched all day;
   Lord, how I did admire it!   *Chorus*

3. With corn and hog fat for my food,
   And digging, guarding, drilling,
   I got as thin as twice-skimmed milk,
   And was scarcely worth the killing.
   And now I'm used to homely fare,
   My skin as tough as leather,
   I do guard duty cheerfully
   In every kind of weather.   *Chorus*

4. I'm brimful of fight, my boys,
   I would not give a "thank ye"
   For all the smiles the girls can give
   Until I've killed a Yankee.
   High private is glorious rank,
   There's wide room for promotion;
   I'll get a corporal's stripes some day,
   When fortune's in the notion.   *Chorus*

5. 'Tis true I have not seen a fight,
   Nor have I smelt gunpowder,
   But then the way I'll pepper them
   Will be a sin to chowder.
   A sergeant's stripes I now will sport,
   Perhaps be color-bearer,
   And then a captain-good for me
   I'll be a regular tearer.   *Chorus*

6. I'll then begin to wear the stars,
   And then the wreaths of glory,
   Until the army I command,
   And poets sing my story.
   Our Congress will pass votes of thanks
   To him who rose from zero,
   The people in a mass will shout,
   Hurrah, behold the hero!   *Chorus*

He fires his gun by accident

7. What's that? oh dear! A boiler's burst,
   A gaspipe has exploded,
   Maybe the Yankees are hard by
   With muskets ready loaded.
   Oh, gallant soldiers, beat 'em back,
   I'll join you in the frolic,
   But I've a chill from head to foot,
   And symptoms of the colic.   *Chorus*

Cumberland Gap

September 17, 1862 ("September mornin' in sixty-two"), the battle of Antietam took place. After the bloody encounter, a Confederate officer asked a straggler from Georgia to explain his absence from the fight. The reply: "I had no shoes. I tried it barefoot, but somehow my feet wouldn't callous. They just kept bleeding. I found it so hard to keep up that though I had the heart of a patriot, I began to feel I didn't have patriotic feet. Of course, I could have crawled on my hands and knees, but then my hands would have got so sore I couldn't have fired my rifle."

2. The first white man in Cumberland Gap,
The first white man in Cumberland Gap,
The first white man in Cumberland Gap,
Was Doctor Walker, an English chap.

3. Daniel Boone on Pinnacle Rock...
He killed Indians with an old flintlock.

4. Cumberland Gap is a noted place...
Three kinds water to wash your face.

5. Cumberland Gap with its cliff and rocks...
Home of the panther, bear, and fox.

6. September mornin' in sixty-two...
Morgan's Yankees all withdrew.

7. They spiked Long Tom on the mountain top...
And over the cliffs they let him drop.

8. They burned the hay, the meal, and the meat...
And left the Rebels nothing to eat.

9. Braxton Bragg with his Rebel band...
He run George Morgan to the blue-grass land.

10. The Rebels now will give a little yell...
They'll scare the Yankees all to Hell.

11. Ol' Aunt Dinah, ef you don't keer...
Leave my little jug settin' right here.

12. Ef it's not here when I come back,
I'll raise Hell in Cumberland Gap.

13. Ol' Aunt Dinah took a little spell...
Broke my little jug all to Hell.

14. I've got a woman in Cumberland Gap...
She's got a boy that calls me "pap."

15. Me and my wife and my wife's grand' pap,
All raise Hell in Cumberland Gap.

There Was An Old Soldier

old to‑bac‑co box. He al‑ways kept to‑bac‑co in his old to‑bac‑co box.

2. Said one old soldier, "Won't you give me a chew?"
   Said the other old soldier, "I'll be hanged if I do,
   Just save up your money and put away your rocks,
   And you'll always have tobacco in your old tobacco box,
   And you'll always have tobacco in your old tobacco box."

3. Well, the one old soldier, he was feeling mighty bad,
   He said, "I'll get even, I will begad!"
   He goes to a corner, takes a rifle from the peg,
   And stabs the other soldier with a splinter from his leg,
   And stabs the other soldier with a splinter from his leg.

4. Now there was an old hen and she had a wooden foot,
   And she made her nest by the mulberry root,
   She laid more eggs than any hen on the farm,
   And another wooden leg wouldn't do her any harm.
   And another wooden leg wouldn't do her any harm.

Johnny Is My Darling

Charlie is my darling, my darling, my darling,
Charlie is my darling, the young chevalier.

This Scottish Jacobite song about Bonnie Prince Charlie served as a model for the Civil
War parody.

Words by Father Reed
Music: "Charlie Is My Darling"

morn – ing, The bright – est of the year, When
John – ny came to my _____ town, A Un – ion Vol – un – teer.

D.S. al Fine

2. As he came marching up the street,
   The bands played loud and clear;
   And everyone came out to greet
   The Union Volunteer. *Chorus*

3. With proudly waving starry flags
   And hearts that knew no fear;
   He came to fight for Freedom's rights,
   A Union Volunteer. *Chorus*

4. But though he's gone to glory win,
   And I left lonely here,
   He'll soon return to me again
   As *Cupid's Volunteer*. *Chorus*

When Johnny Comes Marching Home

Patrick S. Gilmore was bandmaster of the Union Army in New Orleans. The definite Irish quality of this song is no doubt due to Gilmore's Irish birth. However, no firm evidence has ever been produced that would conclusively show a specific Irish antecedent to "Johnny." What we do know for certain is that soldiers in both armies sang and identified with Johnny.

Words and music by Patrick S. Gilmore

2. The old church bell will peal with joy,
   Hurrah, hurrah!
   To welcome home our darling boy,
   Hurrah, hurrah!
   The village lads and lassies say,
   With roses they will strew the way,
   And we'll all feel gay when Johnny comes
   marching home.

3. Get ready for the Jubilee,
   Hurrah, hurrah!
   We'll give the hero three times three,
   Hurrah, hurrah!
   The laurel wreath is ready now
   To place upon his loyal brow,
   And we'll all feel gay when Johnny comes
   marching home.

4. Let love and friendship on that day,
   Hurrah, hurrah!
   Their choicest treasures then display,
   Hurrah, hurrah!
   And let each one perform some part,
   To fill with joy the warrior's heart,
   And we'll all feel gay when Johnny comes
   marching home.

The Rebel Soldier

O Polly dear, O Polly,
The rout has now begun,
And we must march away
At the beating of the drum....

This British soldier was off to "High Germany" in the Seven Years' War (1756–1763). The folk memory runs long and deep.

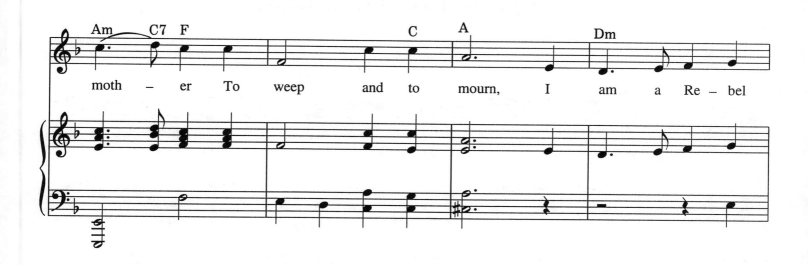

moth - er To weep and to mourn, I am a Re - bel

sol - dier __ And far ____ from my home. _____

2. It's grape shot and musket,
   And the cannons lumber loud,
   There's many a mangled body,
   The blanket for their shroud;
   There's many a mangled body
   Left on the fields alone,
   I am a Rebel soldier
   And far from my home.

3. I'll eat when I'm hungry,
   I'll drink when I am dry,
   If the Yankees don't kill me,
   I'll live until I die;
   If the Yankees don't kill me
   And cause me to mourn,
   I am a Rebel soldier
   And far from my home.

4. Here's a good old cup of brandy
   And a glass of nice wine,
   You can drink to your true love,
   And I will drink to mine;
   And you can drink to your true love,
   And I'll lament and mourn,
   I am a Rebel soldier
   And far from my home.

5. I'll build me a castle on the mountain,
   On some green mountain high,
   Where I can see Polly
   As she is passing by;
   Where I can see Polly
   And help her to mourn,
   I am a Rebel soldier
   And far from my home.

The Southern Soldier

I'll place my knap–sack on my back, My ri – fle on my shoul – der, I'll

march a – way to the fir – ing line, And kill that Yan – kee sol – dier, And

kill that Yan–kee sol – dier, I'll march a way to the fir–ing line And kill that Yan-kee sol – dier.

2. I'll bid farewell to my wife and child,
   Farewell to my aged mother.
   And go and join in the bloody strife,
   Till this cruel war is over,
   Till this cruel war is over,
   I'll go and join in the bloody strife,
   Till this cruel war is over.

3. If I am shot on the battlefield,
   And I should not recover,
   Oh, who will protect my wife and child,
   And care for my aged mother?
   And care for my aged mother,
   Oh, who will protect my wife and child,
   And care for my aged mother?

4. And if our Southern cause is lost,
   And Southern right denied us,
   We'll be ground beneath the tyrant's heel
   For our demands of justice,
   For our demands of justice,
   We'll be ground beneath the tyrant's heel
   For our demands of justice.

5. Before the South shall bow her head,
   Before the tyrants harm us,
   I'll give my all to the Southern cause,
   And die in the Southern army,
   And die in the Southern army,
   I'll give my all to the Southern cause,
   And die in the Southern army.

6. If I must die for my home and land,
   My spirit will not falter,
   Oh, here's my heart and here's my hand
   Upon my country's altar,
   Upon my country's altar,
   Oh, here's my heart and here's my hand
   Upon my country's altar.

7. Then Heaven be with us in the strife,
   Be with the Southern soldier,
   We'll drive the mercenary border,
   Beyond our Southern border,
   Beyond our Southern border,
   We'll drive the mercenary horde
   Beyond our Southern border.

Pat Murphy of the Irish Brigade

Despite the heroism of the New York 69th ("The Fighting Irish"), the Irish were the most under-represented group in proportion to population in the Union Army. However, Irish-influenced song was well represented.

162

163

2. The morning soon broke and poor Paddy awoke,
   He found Rebels to give satisfaction,
   And the drummers were beating the Devil's sad tune,
   They were calling the boys into action. *Chorus*

3. Sure, the day after battle, the dead lay in heaps,
   And Pat Murphy lay bleeding and gory,
   With a hole through his head by some enemy's ball
   That ended his passion for glory. *Chorus*

4. No more in the camp will his letters be read,
   Or his song be heard singing so gaily,
   But he died far away from the friends that he loved,
   And far from the land of shillelagh. *Chorus*

I Can Whip the Scoundrel

Union Major Abner Small (no relation to "Abner" in this song) was taken prisoner on August 18, 1865, near Petersburg, Virginia. As he was being escorted to the rear by a young Confederate soldier, Union shells began bursting all around them. At one point the guard halted, and looking Major Abner straight in the face said, "Yank, I'm damned sorry you didn't capture me."

lay ten dol – lars down, Or twen–ty if you choose, For

I can whip the scoun- drel that stole old Ab – ner's shoes.

2. Jeff Davis was a gentleman,
Abe Lincoln was a fool.
Jeff Davis rode a dapple gray,
Abe Lincoln rode a mule. *Chorus*

3. The Yankees took me prisoner,
They used me rough, it's true;
They took from me my knapsack,
And stole my blankets too. *Chorus*

4. The Yankees took me prisoner,
And if I can get parole,
I'll go right back and fight them,
I will, upon my soul. *Chorus*

Here's Your Mule

Mary Bayard Clark, writing in *The Land We Love* (June 1867) tells how Aunt Abby came to Raleigh one day in April 1865 in search of her "crap critter" that had been "liberated" by Sherman's army.

The Union Provost Marshall was not quite sure what it was that she was after. After a somewhat confused conversation which led him to believe that she was searching for her cow, Aunt Abby exploded: "Lord sakes, who but a Yankee ever heard tell o' tending of a crap with a cow; it's a mule, man, that I'm arter, not a cow."

Words: anonymous
Music by C. D. Benson

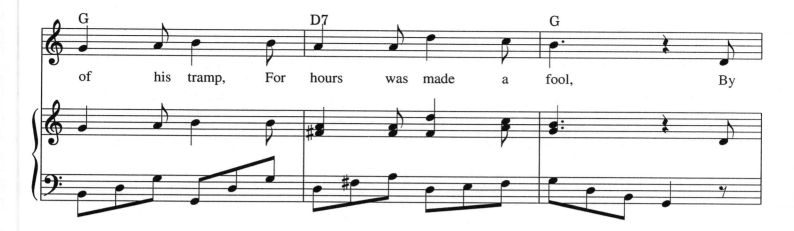

of his tramp, For hours was made a fool, By

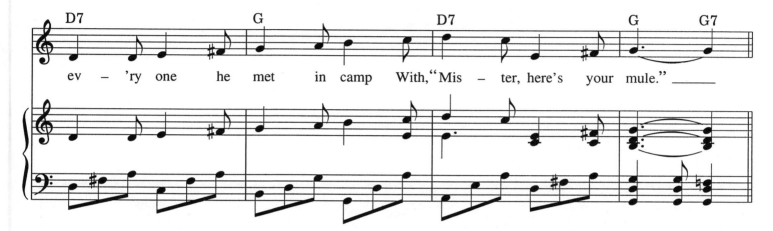

ev – 'ry one he met in camp With, "Mis – ter, here's your mule." ____

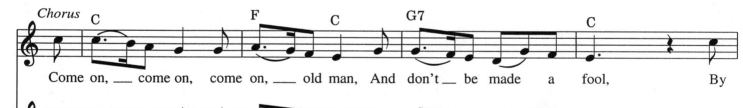

Chorus

Come on, __ come on, come on, __ old man, And don't __ be made a fool, By

ev – 'ry – one you meet in camp With, "Mis – ter, here's your mule." ____

2. His eggs and chickens all were gone,
   Before the break of day;
   The mule was heard of all along,
   That's what the soldiers say;
   And still he hunted all day long,
   Alas! a witless tool,
   Whilst every man would sing the song
   Of, "Mister, here's your mule." *Chorus*

3. The soldiers run in laughing mood,
   On mischief were intent;
   They lifted muley on their back,
   Around from tent to tent;
   Through this hole and that, they pushed
   His head and made a rule,
   To shout with hum'rous voices all,
   "I say! Mister, here's your mule." *Chorus*

4. Alas, one day the mule was missed!
   Ah, who could tell his fate?
   The farmer, like a man bereft,
   Searched early and searched late,
   And as he passed from camp to camp,
   With stricken face – the fool,
   Cried out to ev'ryone he met,
   "Oh, Mister, where's my mule?" *Chorus*

Battles

Cairo

There was never a battle at Cairo, Illinois. In the summer of 1861, the Confederates were planning an attack on this key river city, located at the confluence of the Ohio and Mississippi rivers. Major General John C. Fremont recognized Cairo's military significance, and when he got wind of the Confederate plans he had reinforcements brought in to secure the city. As a result, the Confederates never attacked, and Cairo remained a secure Union outpost for the duration of the war.

Words: anonymous
Music: "White Cockade"

Ca – i – ro, Oh, ___ Ca – i – ro! There's no giv – ing that the ___

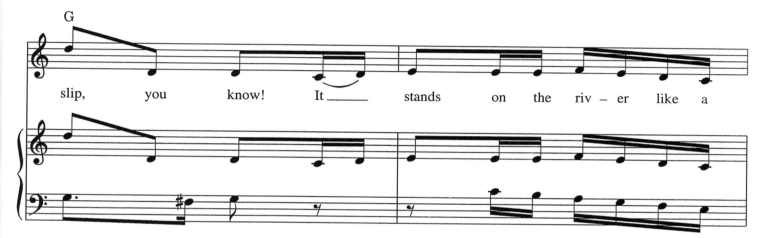

slip, you know! It ___ stands on the riv – er like a

mi – li – ta – ry crow, To take corn ___ con – tra – band ___ for ___ Ca – i – ro.

2. The rolling Mississippi was a highway free,
   When the people down in Dixie acted honestly;
   But since like plunderers they've cut up so,
   They'll have to pay a floating tax to Ca-i-ro!
     Ca-i-ro, Oh, Ca-i-ro!
     The Southrons say it's a precious go,
     That they can't send a boat for a bit of tow,
     But it has to take an overhaul at Ca-i-ro.

3. The Southern chivaligators now, they say,
   To capture the place are on their way;
   But if they'd take *my* advice they'd never try to go
   Within telescopic range of Ca-i-ro!

   Ca-i-ro, Oh, Ca-i-ro!
   The Union guns are mounted so,
   That if once sighted at a nearby foe,
   They'd make a perfect graveyard of Ca-i-ro.

4. Bold Prentiss holds the chief command,
   And prime Jim Lane is close at hand;
   They are bound by their honors to do nothing slow,
   But to take a river revenue at Ca-i-ro!
     Ca-i-ro, Oh, Ca-i-ro!
     There's no giving that the slip, you know,
     And if down the river the traitors want to go,
     They'll have to get their baggage checked at Ca-i-ro!

Flight of Doodles

"When the 'rebels' had been reinforced by the arch-rebels, Johnston and Jackson, with their wornout but gallant men, and when the Federals with their splendid army had turned and were frantically flying before those same 'rebels,' they cared for nothing but to get away. The flight of that panic-stricken mob has often been described, and by many pens, none however so graphic as that which after treating of their disgraceful race, styled them 'Bull Runners.'…" [*Mrs. Cornelia McDonald, commenting on the Confederate victory and Union rout at the Battle of Bull Run (July 21, 1861) in* **A Diary with Reminiscences of the War and Refugee Life in the Shenandoah Valley, 1860-1865** *(1875)*]

Words: anonymous
Music: "Root Hog or Die"

I_____ come from old Ma – nas – sas with a pock – et full of fun,

I killed for – ty Yan – kees with a sin – gle bar – reled gun; It don't

make a niff – a – stiff-'rence to nei – ther you nor I,

Big Yank – ee, Lit – tle Yank – ee, all _____ run or die.

2. I saw all the Yankees at Bull Run,
   They fought like the devil when the battle first begun.
   But it don't make a niff-a-stiff'rence to neither you nor I,
   They took to their heels, boys, and you ought to see 'em fly.

3. I saw old Fuss-and-Feathers Scott, twenty miles away,
   His horses stuck up their ears, and you ought to hear 'em neigh;
   But it don't make a niff-a-stiff'rence to neither you nor I,
   Old Scott fled like the devil, boys, root, hog, or die.

4. I then saw a "Tiger," from the old Crescent City,
   He cut down the Yankees without any pity;
   Oh! It don't make a diff-a-bitt'rence to neither you nor I,
   We whipped the Yankee boys and made the boobies cry.

5. I saw South Carolina, the first in the cause,
   Shake the dirty Yankees till she broke all their jaws;
   Oh! It don't make a niff-a-stiff'rence to neither you nor I,
   South Carolina give 'em Hell, boys, root, hog, or die.

6. I saw old Virginia, standing firm and true,
   She fought mighty hard to whip the dirty crew;
   Oh! It don't make a niff-a-stiff'rence to neither you nor I,
   Old Virginia's blood and thunder, boys, root, hog, or die.

7. I saw old Georgia, the next in the van,
   She cut down the Yankees almost to a man;
   Oh! It don't make a niff-a-stiff'rence to neither you nor I,
   Georgia's some in a fight, boys, root, hog, or die.

8. I saw Alabama in the midst of the storm,
   She stood like a giant in the contest so warm;
   Oh! It don't make a niff-a-stiff'rence to neither you nor I,
   Alabama fought the Yankees, boys, till the last one did fly.

9. I saw Texas go in with a smile,
   But I tell you what it is, she made the Yankees bile,
   Oh! It don't make a niff-a-stiff'rence to neither you nor I,
   Texas is the devil, boys, root, hog, or die.

10. I saw North Carolina in the deepest of the battle,
    She knocked down the Yankees and made their bones rattle;
    Oh! It don't make a niff-a-stiff'rence to neither you nor I,
    North Carolina's got the grit, boys, root, hog, or die.

11. Old Florida came in with a terrible shout,
    She frightened all the Yankees till their eyes stuck out;
    Oh! It don't make a niff-a-stiff'rence to neither you nor I,
    Florida's death on Yankees, boys, root, hog, or die.

The Battle of Shiloh

The Battle of Shiloh took place over two bloody days, April 6–7, 1862. It pitted Union forces under Grant, Sherman, Prentiss, and others against the Confederates under Bragg, Breckenridge, Polk, and others. It was a carnage that saw 20,000 killed and wounded, about equally distributed between the two sides. Both sides now realized what lay in store for them—a long and terrible war.

176

2. Oh it was on April, the sixteenth day,
   In spite of a long and muddy way,
   We landed safe at Corinth Bay,
   All on our route to Shiloh.

3. That night we lay on the cold ground,
   No tents nor shelters could we find;
   And in the rain we almost drowned,
   All on our way to Shiloh.

4. Next morning a burning sun did rise,
   Beneath the eastern cloudless sky,
   And General Beauregard replied:
   Prepare to march to Shiloh.

5. And when our Shiloh hove in view,
   It would the bravest hearts subdue
   To see the Yankee motley crew
   That held the works at Shiloh.

6. For they were strongly fortified,
   With batteries on the riverside.
   Our generals viewed the plains and cried;
   "We'll get hot work at Shiloh."

7. And when those batteries strove to gain,
   The balls fell around us thick as rain,
   And many a hero there was slain,
   Upon the plains of Shiloh.

8. The thirty-third and the Zouaves,
   They charged the batteries and gave three cheers,
   And General Beauregard rang the airs
   With Southern steel at Shiloh.

9. Their guns and knapsacks they threw down,
   They ran like hares before the hounds.
   The Yankee Dutch could not withstand
   The Southern charge at Shiloh.

10. Now many a pretty maid did mourn
    A lover who'll no more return;
    The cruel war has from her torn
    His body lies at Shiloh.

The Battle of Shiloh Hill

Words by M. B. Smith (Company C, 2d Regiment, Texas Volunteers)
Music: "Wandering Sailor"

2. It was the Sixth of April,
   Just at the break of day,
   The drums and fifes were playing
   For us to march away;
   The feeling of that hour
   I do remember still,
   For the wounded and the dying
   That lay on Shiloh Hill.

3. About the hour of sunrise
   The battle it began,
   And before the day had vanished
   We fought them hand to hand;
   The horrors of the field
   Did my heart with anguish fill,
   For the wounded and the dying
   That lay on Shiloh Hill.

4. There were men from every nation
   Laid on those bloody plains,
   Fathers, sons, and brothers
   Were numbered with the slain,
   That has caused so many homes
   With deep mourning to be filled,
   All from the bloody battle
   That was fought on Shiloh Hill.

5. The wounded men were crying
   For help from everywhere,
   While others, who were dying,
   Were offering God their prayer,
   "Protect my wife and children
   If it is Thy holy will!"
   Such were the prayers I heard
   That night on Shiloh Hill.

6. And early the next morning
   We were called to arms again,
   Unmindful of the wounded
   And unmindful of the slain,
   The struggle was renewed
   And ten thousand men were killed;
   This was the second conflict
   Of the famous Shiloh Hill.

7. The battle it raged on,
   Though dead and dying men
   Lay thick all o'er the ground,
   On the hill and on the glen;
   And from their deadly wounds
   The blood ran like a rill;
   Such were the mournful sights
   That I saw on Shiloh Hill.

8. Before the day was ended
   The battle ceased to roar,
   And thousands of brave soldiers
   Had fell to rise no more;
   They left their vacant ranks
   For some other ones to fill,
   And now their mouldering bodies
   All lie on Shiloh Hill.

9. And now my song is ended
   About those bloody plains,
   I hope the sight by mortal man
   May ne'er be seen again;
   But I pray to God, the Saviour,
   "If consistent with Thy will,
   To save the souls of all who fell
   On bloody Shiloh Hill."

The Cumberland and the Merrimac

"A Yankee cheesebox on a raft," they named our little boat,
I'm sure no better box of cheese was ever set afloat;
For catching rats we bait with cheese, for rebels do the same,
And if they'll only take the bait we'll surely catch our game.

The end of an era took place on March 8, 1862. The first ironclad naval vessel, the Confederate *Virginia,* known to history as the *Merrimac* (it had been the name of a sunken U.S. frigate which the Confederates had raised and rebuilt) sank the Union *Cumberland* in Chesapeake Bay. By the very next day, the "Yankee cheesebox on a raft," the *Monitor,* the second ironclad the world had ever seen, steamed out to even the score.

some – thing like a house top,_____ on our lee – ward she does lay."

2. Our captain seized his telescope and he gazed far o'er the blue,
   And then he turned and spoke to his brave and loyal crew,
   "That thing which yonder lies floating, that looks like some turtle's back,
   It's that infernal Rebel steamer, and they call her *Merrimac.*"

3. Our decks were cleared for action and our guns were pointed through,
   But still she kept a-coming up across the water blue,
   And on, still on, she kept coming, till no distance stood apart;
   When she sent a ball a-humming, stilled the beat of many a heart.

4. It was then we fired our broadside into ribs of steel,
   And yet no break in her iron made, no damage did she feel,
   Till at length that Rebel pirate unto our captain spoke,
   Saying, "Haul down your flying colors now, or I'll sink your Yankee boat."

5. Our captain's eyes did glisten and his cheeks turned pale with rage,
   And then in tones of thunder, to that Rebel pirate said:
   "My men are brave and loyal, too, they're true to every man,
   And before I'll strike my colors down, you may sink me in the sand."

6. Well, *The Merrimac* she left us then for a hundred yards or more,
   Then with her whistles screaming out, on our wooden side bore;
   She struck us at our midship, and her ram went crashing through,
   And the water came a-pouring in on our brave and loyal crew.

7. Well, our captain turned unto his men and unto them he did say,
   "I never will strike my colors down while *The Cumberland* rides the wave,
   But I'll go down with my gallant ship for to meet a watery grave,
   And you, my loyal comrades, you may seek your lives to save."

8. They swore they never would leave him, but would man their guns afresh,
   Poured broadside after broadside, till the water reached their breasts;
   And then they sank far down, far down into the watery deep,
   The Stars and Stripes still flying from her mainmast's highest peak.

The Cumberland Crew

When the *Cumberland* went down, 117 men out of a crew of 376 were lost. It was the kind of tragic incident that, apart from it strategic significance, lent itself to being recounted in a narrative ballad.

2. That ill-fated day, about ten in the morning,
   The sky it was cloudless and bright shone the sun;
   The drums of the *Cumberland* sounded a warning
   That told every man to stand by his gun.
   When an iron-clad frigate down on us came bearing,
   High up in the air her base Rebel flag flew;
   An emblem of treason she proudly was wearing,
   Determined to conquer the *Cumberland* crew.

3. They fought us three hours with stern resolution,
   Till those Rebels found cannon could never decide;
   For the flag of Secession had no power to quell them,
   Though the blood from our scuppers did crimson the tide.
   She struck us amidships, our planks she did sever,
   Her sharp iron prow pierced our noble ship through;
   And slowly we sank in Virginia's dark waters,
   "We'll die by our guns," cried the *Cumberland* crew.

4. Oh, slowly she sank in the dark rolling waters,
   Their voices on earth will be heard never more.
   They'll be wept by Columbia's brave sons and fair daughters,
   May their blood be avenged on Virginia's old shore.
   And if ever sailors in battle assemble,
   God bless our dear banner – the red, white, and blue;
   Beneath its proud folds we'll cause tyrants to tremble,
   Or sink at our guns like the *Cumberland* crew.

Virginia's Bloody Soil

The armies of Grant and Lee met head on for a terrible week, from May 5 through May 12, 1864, near the Rapidan River not far from Fredricksburg. It was a heavily wooded area known as The Wilderness. Grant was pushing inexorably toward Richmond; Lee fought back mightily. The battles raged on into June as the Army of the Potomac pushed south. At the end of this seven-week campaign some 65,000 (!) Union soldiers were killed, wounded, or missing. Lee's smaller army had suffered proportionate casualties—35,000.

Slow ad lib.

Come all you loy – al Un – ion–ists, when–ev – er you may be, _____ I hope you'll pay at – ten – tion and lis – ten un – to me; _____ For well you know the blood and woe, the mis – e – ry and toil, _____ It

took to down Se-ces-sion on Vir-gin-ia's blood-y soil.

2. When our good old flag, the Stars and Stripes, from Sumter's walls was hurled,
   And high o'erhead on the forwardest walls the Rebels their flag unfurled,
   It aroused each loyal Northern man and caused his blood to boil
   For to see that flag - Secession's rag - float o'er Virginia's soil.

3. Then from o'er the hills and mountain tops there came that wild alarm:
   Rise up! ye gallant sons of North, our country calls to arms!
   Come from the plains, o'er hill and dale, ye hardy sons of toil,
   For our flag is trampled in the dust on Virginia's bloody soil!

4. And thousands left their native homes, some never to return,
   And many's the wife and family dear were left behind to mourn.
   There was one who went among them who from danger would ne'er recoil;
   Now his bones lie bleaching on the fields of Virginia's bloody soil.

5. In the great fight of the Wilderness, where's many the brave men fell,
   Our captain led his comrades on through Rebel shot and shell;
   The wounded 'round they strewed the ground, the dead lay heaped in piles,
   The comrades weltered in their blood on Virginia's bloody soil.

6. The Rebels fought like fury, or tigers drove to bay;
   They knew full well if the truth they'd tell they could not win the day.
   It was hand to hand they fought 'em, the struggle was fierce and wild,
   Till a bullet pierced our captain's brain on Virginia's bloody soil.

7. And now our hero's sleeping with thousands of the brave;
   No marble slab does mark the place that shows where he was laid.
   He died to save our Union, he's free from care and toil
   Thank God! the Stars and Stripes still wave above Virginia's soil!

Roll, Alabama, Roll

When the war broke out the Confederacy had some experienced naval officers but no navy. In a desperate attempt to break the Union blockade that would surely strangle the South, agents were sent to England and France to try to purchase ships for that purpose. The *Alabama* was one of those ships. It was built in Birkenhead, England, on the river Mersey, not far from Liverpool in 1862. It created havoc with Union shipping, sinking over 50 merchant vessels. On June 19, 1864, the man-of-war *U.S.S. Kearsarge* finally caught up with the *Alabama* off the coast of Cherbourg, France, and after a fierce battle, sent it to a watery grave.

188

2. 'Twas laid in the yard of Jonathan Laird,
   Roll, *Alabama,* roll.
   'Twas laid in the town of Birkenhead,
   Roll, *Alabama,* roll.

3. Down the Mersey ways she rolled then,
   Roll, *Alabama,* roll.
   Liverpool fitted her with guns and men,
   Roll, *Alabama,* roll.

4. From the Western Isles she sailed forth,
   Roll, *Alabama,* roll.
   To destroy the commerce of the North,
   Roll, *Alabama,* roll.

5. To Cherbourg port she sailed one day,
   Roll, *Alabama,* roll.
   To take her count of prize money,
   Roll, *Alabama,* roll.

6. Many a sailor lad he saw his doom,
   Roll, *Alabama,* roll.
   When the *Ke-arsarge* it hove in view,
   Roll, *Alabama,* roll.

7. Till a ball from the forward pivot that day,
   Roll, *Alabama,* roll.
   Shot the *Alabama's* stern away,
   Roll, *Alabama,* roll.

8. Off the three-mile limit in sixty-five,
   Roll, *Alabama,* roll.
   The *Alabama* went to her grave,
   Roll, *Alabama,* roll.

When Sherman Marched Down to the Sea

General Sherman led his 62,000 battle-hardened men through Georgia, from Atlanta to Savannah, in late 1864. Grant and Lincoln had been skeptical about Sherman's chances, but were finally convinced by his eloquence: "...We have a power which Davis cannot resist.... I can make the march, and make Georgia howl!"

Words by S. B. M. Meyers
Music by E. Mack

rid – er came out __ of the dark – ness That hung o – ver moun – tain and

tree, And shout– ed, "Boys! up and be read–y, __ For

Sher – man will march to the sea," And shout– ed, "Boys, up and be

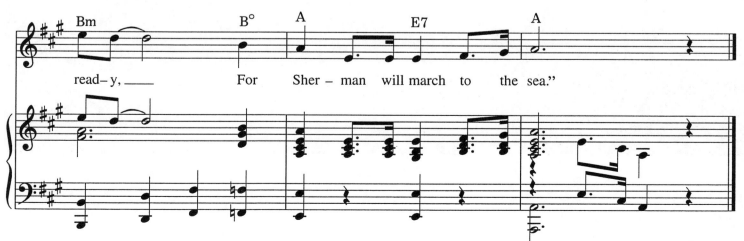

read–y, __ For Sher – man will march to the sea."

2. Then shout upon shout for bold Sherman
   Went up from each valley and glen;
   And the bugles re-echoed the music
   That rose from the lips of the men;
   For we know that the stars in our banners
   More bright in their splendor would be,
   And that blessings from North land would greet us,
   When Sherman marched down to the sea;
   And that blessings from North land would greet us,
   When Sherman marched down to the sea.

3. Then forward, boys, forward to battle,
   We marched on our wearisome way;
   And we stormed the wild hills of Resacca,
   God bless those who fell on that day!
   Then Kenesaw, dark in its glory,
   Frowned down on the flag of the free,
   But the East and the West bore our standards,
   When Sherman marched down to the sea;
   But the East and the West bore our standards,
   When Sherman marched down to the sea.

4. Still onward we pressed till our banners
   Swept out from Atlanta's grim walls,
   And the blood of the patriot dampened
   The soil where the Traitor flag falls.
   We paused not to weep for the fallen,
   That slept by each river and tree,
   But we twined them a wreath of the laurel,
   When Sherman marched down to the sea;
   But we twined them a wreath of the laurel,
   When Sherman marched down to the sea.

5. Proud, proud was our army that morning,
   That stood where the pine darkly towers,
   When Sherman said, "Boys, you are weary,
   But today, fair Savannah is ours."
   Then we all sang a song for our Chieftain,
   That echoed o'er river and lea,
   And the stars on our banners shone brighter,
   When Sherman marched down to the sea;
   And the stars on our banners shone brighter,
   When Sherman marched down to the sea.

A Life on the Vicksburg Bluff

When the Union Army captured Vicksburg on July 4, 1863, after a two-month siege, they found a Confederate garrison so weak and malnourished that Grant issued them a five-day ration from Federal stores. The starving Confederates had been reduced to eating mule meat ("Logan's beef") and pea bread. A soldier in the Third Louisiana Regiment, A. Dalsheimer, chose the rollicking old tune "A Life on the Ocean Wave" to describe, in rather light-hearted terms, what were in reality ghastly conditions.

Words by A. Dalsheimer
Music: "A Life on the Ocean Wave"

A life on the Vicks — burg bluff, _____ A ___ home in the trench— es deep, _____ where we

dodge Yank shells e - nough, _____ And our old pea— bread _ won't keep. _____ On "old

Lo - gan's" beef I pine, _____ For there's fat on his bones no more; _____ Oh!

193

give me some pork and brine,_____ And truck from a sut – ler's store._____ A

Chorus

life on the Vicks – burg bluff,_____ A ____ home in the trench – es deep,_____ Where we

dodge Yank shells e – nough,_____ And our old pea – bread_ won't keep._____ Pea–

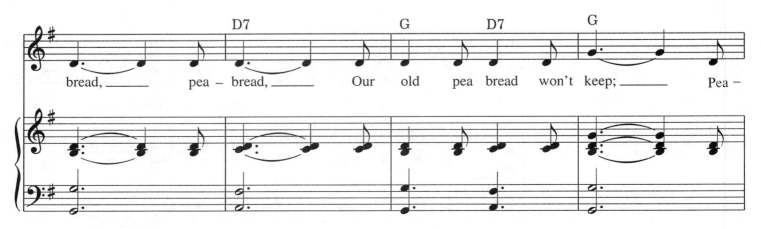

bread, _____ pea – bread,_____ Our old pea bread won't keep; _____ Pea–

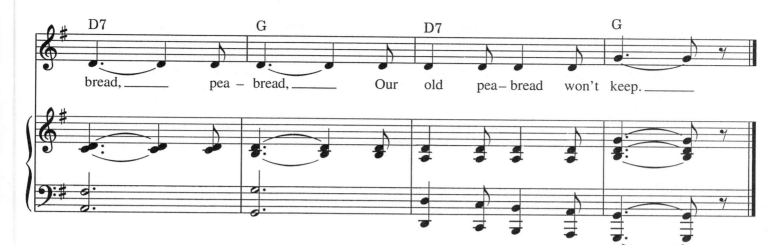

bread, _____ pea – bread, _____ Our old pea – bread won't keep. _____

2. Old Grant is starving us out,
   Our grub is fast wasting away,
   Pemb' don't know what he's about,
   And he hasn't for many a day,
   So we'll bury "old Logan" tonight,
   From tough beef we'll be set free;
   We'll put him far out of sight,
   No more of his meat for me. *Chorus*

3. Texas steers are no longer in view,
   Mule steaks are now "done up brown,"
   While pea-bread, mule roast and mule stew,
   Are our fare in Vicksburg town;
   And the song of our hearts shall be,
   While the Yanks and their gunboats rave;
   A life in a bomb-proof for me,
   And a tear on "old Logan's" grave. *Chorus*

4. Like a rebel caged I pine,
   And I dodge when the cannons roar;
   But give me corn dodgers and swine,
   And I'll stay forever more.
   Once more in the trench I stand,
   With my own far-ranging gun;
   Should the fray come hand to hand,
   I'll wager my rations I run. *Chorus*

5. The trench is no longer in view;
   The shells have begun to fall;
   'Tis a sound I hate – don't you?
   Into my rat-hole I'll crawl.
   The bullets may whistle by,
   The terrible bombs come down;
   But give me full rations, and I
   Will stay in my hole in the ground. *Chorus*

The Fall of Charleston

Turning northward from Savannah, Sherman marched his men toward Charleston, South Carolina, which was taken on April 17, 1865. He met his Confederate counterpart, Major General John C. Breckenridge, to discuss terms of surrender. Breckenridge was a brilliant lawyer who attempted to dazzle Sherman with his seemingly boundless knowledge of international and constitutional law, and of the laws of war—international wars, civil wars, and wars of rebellion.

After a while all this erudition got to Sherman, who pushed back his chair and exclaimed: "See here, gentlemen, who is doing this surrendering anyhow? If this thing goes on, you'll have me sending a letter of apology to Jeff Davis."

Words by Eugene T. Johnson
Music: "Whack Row De Dow"

2. The South Carolina chivalry,
   They once did loudly boast
   That the footsteps of a Union man
   Should ne'er pollute their coast.
   They'd fight the Yankees two to
     one,
   Who only fought for booty;
   But when the "mudsills" came along,
   It was "Legs do your duty!"
     With a whack row de dow!
     Babylon is fallen;
     Whack row de dow,
     The end is drawing near.

3. And from the "Sacred City,"
   This valiant warlike throng
   Skedaddled in confusion,
   Although thirty thousand strong –
   Without a shot, without a blow,
   Or least sign of resistance,
   And leaving their poor friends
     behind,
   With the "Yankees" for assistance.
     With a whack row de dow!
     How are you Southern chivalry?
     Whack row de dow!
     Your race is nearly run.

4. And again o'er Sumter's battered
     walls,
   The Stars and Stripes do fly,
   While the Chivalry of Sixty-One
   In the "last ditch" lie;
   With Sherman, Grant, and Porter,
     too,
   To lead our men to glory;
   We'll squash poor Jeff's Confederacy,
   And then get "Hunkydory."
     With a whack row de dow!
     How are you neutral Johnny Bull?
     Whack row de dow!
     We'll settle next with you.

Brother Green

The war divided many families. Brother literally fought brother. In *The Soldiers' and Sailors' Half-Dime Tales of the Late Rebellion* (1868), the tale is told of a Confederate picket calling out across the Rappahannock to a Union guard stationed on the opposing bank. He asked what Union regiment was posted there, and when informed that it was a particular Pennsylvania outfit, requested that his brother Harry come down to the edge of the river....

"So Harry went down and through, contrary to orders, to the rebel side of the river and had a talk with his brother. Returning, after a while, to his own side, he went 'on post' opposite to him and watched him as closely as if he were some stranger rebel. Truly, queer events grew out of this war."

Words: anonymous
Music: "Barbara Allen"
Plaintively ♩ = 80

2. The Southern foe has laid me low,
   On this cold ground to suffer,
   Dear brother stay, and put me away,
   And write my wife a letter.

3. Tell her I know she's prayed for me,
   And now her prayers are answered,
   That I might be prepared to die
   If I should fall in battle.

4. Go tell my wife she must not grieve,
   Go kiss my little children,
   For I am going to Heaven to live
   To see my dear old mother.

5. Dear sister may have gone there, too,
   She lives and reigns with angels,
   And Jeffer's son who died when young,
   I know I'll see their faces.

6. I have one brother in this wide world,
   He's fighting for the Union,
   But oh, dear wife, I've lost my life,
   To put down this Rebellion.

7. Tell my wife she must not grieve,
   And kiss the little children,
   For they will call their pa in vain,
   When he is up in Heaven.

8. My little babes, I love them well,
   Oh could I once more see them,
   That I might give a long farewell
   And meet them all in Heaven.

199

Negro Spirituals & Abolitionist Songs

Go Down, Moses

It was only natural that the Negro slave should identify with the prophets and heroes in the Bible. Moses, leading the children of Israel out of bondage and toward the promised land, was a natural and powerful symbol. Ex-slave Harriet Tubman may very well have been the actual "Moses" of the song. As a tireless conductor on the Underground Railroad, she made scores of journeys into slavery's "Egypt land," returning north each time with a group of runaway slaves.

Tell ol' Phar – aoh, To let my peo–ple go.

2. Thus saith the Lord, bold Moses said,
   Let my people go,
   If not, I'll smite your first-born dead,
   Let my people go. *Chorus*

3. No more shall they in bondage toil,
   Let them come out with Egypt's spoil. *Chorus*

4. The Lord told Moses what to do,
   To lead the Hebrew children through. *Chorus*

5. O come along Moses, you'll not get lost,
   Stretch out your rod and come across. *Chorus*

6. As Israel stood by the waterside,
   At God's command it did divide. *Chorus*

7. When they reached the other shore,
   They sang a song of triumph o'er. *Chorus*

8. Pharaoh said he'd go across,
   But Pharaoh and his host were lost. *Chorus*

9. Jordan shall stand up like a wall,
   And the walls of Jericho shall fall. *Chorus*

10. Your foes shall not before you stand,
    And you'll possess fair Canaan's Land. *Chorus*

11. O let us all from bondage flee,
    And let us all in Christ be free. *Chorus*

12. We need not always weep and mourn,
    And wear these slavery chains forlorn. *Chorus*

Follow the Drinking Gourd

The Drinking Gourd was the Big Dipper, whose handle pointed north—to freedom. As the story goes, the "little river" met the "great big river" (the Ohio River), which led to Pennsylvania and, eventually, safe haven in Canada. The "peg foot" may have belonged to a one-legged sailor, "Peg Leg Joe," who was a conductor on the Underground Railroad.

Words and music adapted and arranged by Lee Hays
and the Weavers from a traditional song

follow the drink – in' gourd. When the gourd.

When the gourd.

2. The riverbank will make a very good road,
   The dead trees show you the way,
   Left foot, peg foot, traveling on
   Follow the drinking gourd.   *Chorus*

3. The river ends between two hills,
   Follow the drinking gourd,
   There's another river on the other side,
   Follow the drinking gourd.   *Chorus*

4. Where the great big river meets the little river,
   Follow the drinking gourd,
   The old man is a-waitin' for to carry you to freedom,
   If you follow the drinking gourd.   *Chorus*

Many Thousand Gone

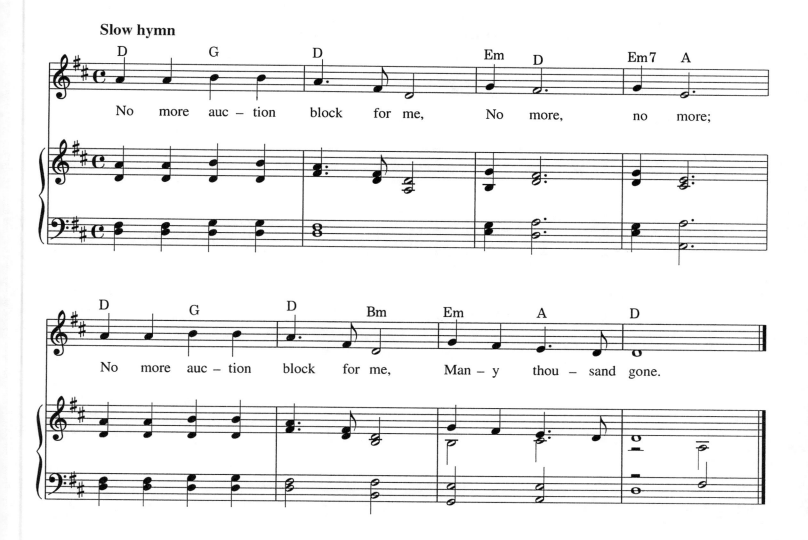

Slow hymn

No more auc – tion block for me, No more, no more;

No more auc – tion block for me, Man – y thou – sand gone.

2. No more peck of corn for me,
   No more, no more;
   No more peck of corn for me,
   Many thousand gone.

3. No more driver's lash for me...

4. No more pint o' salt for me...

5. No more hundred lash for me...

6. No more mistress' call for me...

Clear the Track

In 1844, Jesse Hutchinson, a member of the famous Singing Hutchinson Family of New Hampshire—a staunchly militant Abolitionist group—wrote the words to this song, using Daniel Emmett's tune "Old Dan Tucker." The Hutchinsons were the musical voice of the pre–Civil War Abolitionist movement, writing and performing scores of fiery "protest" songs for over a quarter century.

Words: Jesse Hutchinson
Music: "Old Dan Tucker" (by Daniel D. Emmett)

Ho, the car E—man—ci—pa—tion Rides ma—jes—tic through the na—tion,

Bear—ing on its train the sto—ry, Li—ber—ty! a na—tion's glo—ry.

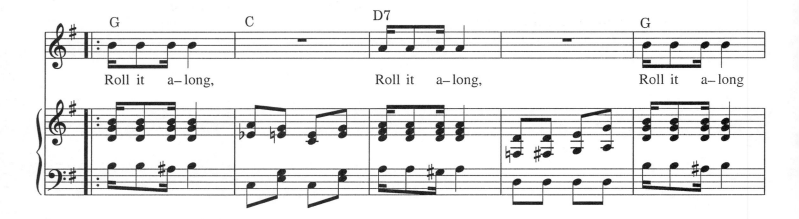

Roll it a—long, Roll it a—long, Roll it a—long

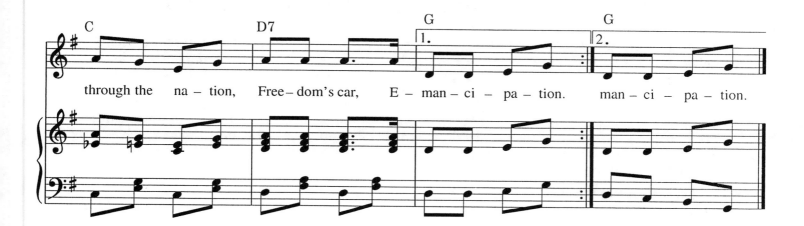

through the na – tion, Free – dom's car, E – man – ci – pa – tion. man – ci – pa – tion.

2. Men of various predilections,
   Frightened, run in all directions;
   Merchants, Editors, Physicians,
   Lawyers, Priests and Politicians.
     Get out of the way! (3) Every station, ⎦2
     Clear the track for 'mancipation.

3. All true friends of Emancipation,
   Haste to Freedom's Railroad Station;
   Quick into the cars get seated,
   All is ready and completed.
     Put on the steam! (3) All are crying, ⎦2
     And the Liberty Flags are flying.

4. Now again the Bell is tolling,
   Soon you'll see the car wheels rolling;
   Hinder not their destination,
   Chartered for Emancipation.
     Wood up the fire! (3) Keep it flashing, ⎦2
     While the train goes onward dashing.

5. Hear the mighty car wheel's humming!
   Now look out! *The Engine's coming!*
   Church and Statesmen! Hear the thunder!
   Clear the track! All are singing,
     Get off the track! (3) All are singing, ⎦2
     While the Liberty Bell is ringing.

6. On triumphant, see them bearing,
   Through sectarian rubbish tearing;
   The Bell and Whistle and the Steaming
   Startles thousands from their dreaming.
     Look out for the cars! (3) While the Bell rings, ⎦2
     Ere the sound your funeral knell rings.

7. See the people run to meet us;
   At the depots thousands greet us;
   All take seats with exultation,
   In the car Emancipation.
     Huzza! Huzza! (3) Emancipation ⎦2
     Soon will bless our happy nation.

We Wait Beneath the Furnace Blast

Despite their identification with the cause of the Union, the Hutchinsons often found them-selves at odds with Union military brass, who were often less than enthusiastic about the message of Abolition. In an 1862 concert tour among the troops of the Army of the Potomac, they so incensed General Kearny that he canceled all further performances of theirs. He had taken particular exception to "We Wait Beneath the Furnace Blast." The controversy went up the chain of command until it was finally brought before Lincoln himself, who said, "It is just the character of song that I desire the soldiers to hear." The matter was resolved by a compromise which allowed the Hutchinsons to perform before troops only when invited by specific commanders.

Words by John Greenleaf Whittier
Music: "Ein Feste Burg" (by Martin Luther)

Chorale Arrangement by J. S. Bach

2. The hand-breadth cloud the sages feared,
   Its bloody rain is dropping;
   The poison plant the fathers spared,
   All else is overtopping.
     East, West, South, North,
     It curses the Earth;
     All justice dies,
     And fraud and lies
   Live only in its shadow.

3. What gives the wheat fields blades of steel?
   What points the Rebel cannon?
   What sets the roaring rabble's heel
   On the old star-spangled pennon?
     What breaks the oath
     Of the men of the South?
     What whets the knife
     For the Union's life?
   Hark to the answer: SLAVERY!

4. Then waste no blows on lesser foes,
   In strife unworthy freemen;
   God lifts today the veil, and shows
   The features of the demon!
     O North and South,
     Its victims both,
     Can ye not cry,
     "Let Slavery die!"
   And Union find in freedom?

5. What though the cast-out spirit tear
   Then nation in his going?
   We who have shared the guilt must share
   The pang of his o'erthrowing!
     Whate'er the loss,
     Whate'er the cross,
     Shall they complain
     Of present pain,
   Who trust in God's hereafter?

6. For who that leans on His right arm
   Was ever yet forsaken?
   What righteous cause can suffer harm
   If He its part has taken?
     Though wild and loud,
     And dark the cloud,
     Behind its folds
     His hand upholds
   The calm sky of tomorrow.

7. Above the maddening cry for blood,
   Above the wild war-drumming,
   Let Freedom's voice be heard, with good
   The evil overcoming.
     Give prayer and purse
     To stay The Curse,
     Whose wrong we share,
     Whose shame we bear,
   Whose end shall gladden heaven!

8. In vain the bells of war shall ring
   Of triumphs and revenges,
   While still is spared the evil thing
   That severs and estranges.
     But blest the ear
     That yet shall hear
     The jubilant bell
     That rings the knell
   Of Slavery forever!

9. Then let the selfish lip be dumb,
   And hushed the breath of sighing;
   Before the joy of peace must come
   The pains of purifying.
     God give us grace,
     Each in his place
     To bear his lot,
     And murmuring not,
   Endure, and wait, and labor!

Steal Away

Coded language has always been a means of communication by oppressed people in the face of their oppressors. A seemingly innocuous phrase like "steal away to Jesus" could and did convey information about a secret meeting of slaves or an escape attempt.

Very slow ad lib.

2. Green trees are bending,
   Poor sinner stands a-trembling;
   The trumpet sounds within-a my soul,
   I ain't got long to stay here. *Chorus*

3. Tombstones are bursting,
   Poor sinner stands a-trembling;
   The trumpet sounds within-a my soul,
   I ain't got long to stay here. *Chorus*

4. My Lord calls me,
   He calls me by the lightning;
   The trumpet sounds within-a my soul,
   I ain't got long to stay here. *Chorus*

My Father, How Long?

The next six spirituals speak (sing) for themselves. They express the despair, the longing, the militancy, and finally the joy of the people who lived through those terrible times.

2. We'll soon be free,
   We'll soon be free,
   We'll soon be free,
   The Lord will call us home. *Chorus*

3. We'll walk the miry road,
   Where pleasure never dies. *Chorus*

4. We'll walk the golden streets,
   Of the new Jerusalem. *Chorus*

5. My brothers do sing,
   The praises of the Lord. *Chorus*

6. We'll fight for liberty,
   When the Lord will call us home. *Chorus*

Slavery Chain Done Broke At Last

Words: anonymous
Music: "Joshua Fit the Battle of Jericho"

2. I did tell him how I suffer,
   In the dungeon and the chain;
   And the days I went with head bowed down,
   An' my broken flesh and pain. *Chorus*

3. I did know my Jesus heard me,
   'Cause the spirit spoke to me,
   An' said, "Rise my chile, your children
   An' you too shall be free." *Chorus*

4. I done p'int one mighty captain
   For to marshall all my hosts;
   An' to bring my bleeding ones to me,
   An' not one shall be lost. *Chorus*

5. Now no more weary trav'lin',
   'Cause my Jesus set me free,
   An' there's no more auction block for me
   Since He give me liberty. *Chorus*

The Gold Band

Goin' to march a — way in the gold band, In the ar — my, bye and bye; Goin' to march a — way in the gold band, In the gold band, In the ar — my, bye and bye. Sin — ner,

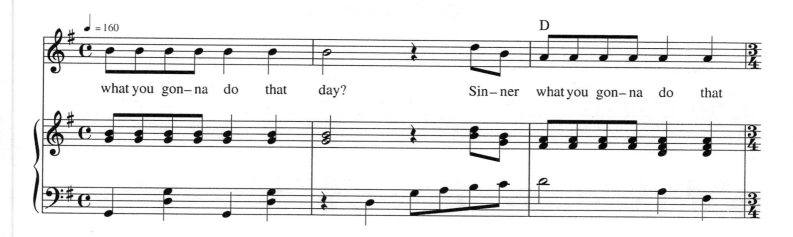

what you gon–na do that day? Sin–ner what you gon–na do that

day? When the fire's a — roll — ing be–

hind you, In the ar – my, bye and bye.

2. Sister Mary goin' to hand down the robe,
   In the army, bye and bye;
   Goin' to hand down the robe and the gold band,
   In the army, bye and bye. *Chorus*

Oh, Freedom

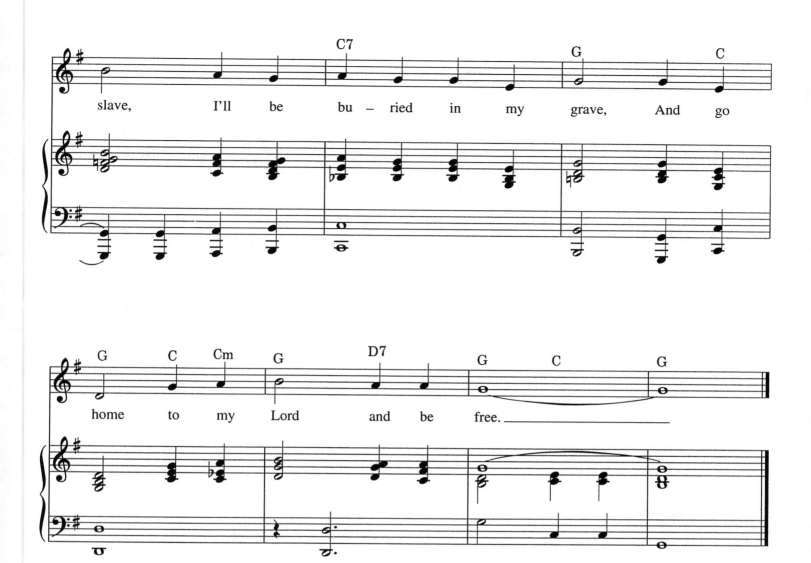

slave, I'll be bu – ried in my grave, And go

home to my Lord and be free. _____

2. No more moaning, no more moaning,
   No more moaning over me.
   And before I'll be a slave,
   I'll be buried in my grave,
   And go home to my Lord and be free.

3. No more weeping, etc.

4. There'll be singing, etc.

221

Free At Last

Way down yon-der in the grave-yard walk, I thank God I'm free at last,

Me and my Je-sus gon-na meet and talk, ____ I thank God I'm free at last. Oh

D. C. al Fine

2. On my knees when the light passed by,
   I thank God I'm free at last,
   Thought my soul would rise and fly,
   I thank God I'm free at last. *Chorus*

3. Some of these mornings, bright and fair,
   I thank God I'm free at last,
   Gonna meet my Jesus in the middle of the air,
   I thank God I'm free at last. *Chorus*

The Lighter Side

Sixty-Three Is the Jubilee

Abraham Lincoln signed the final draft of the Emancipation Proclamation on New Year's Day, 1863: "Fellow citizens, we cannot escape history.... In *giving* freedom to the *slave,* we *assure* freedom to the *free....*"

Words by J. L. Greene
Music by D. A. French

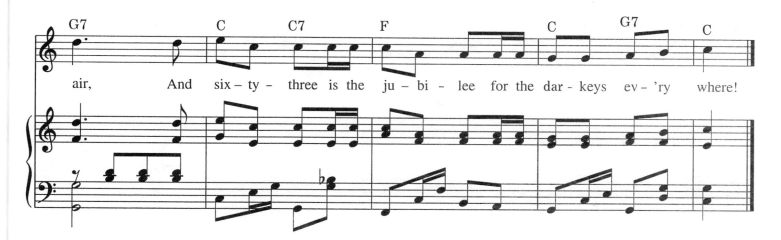

air, And six-ty – three is the ju-bi-lee for the dar-keys ev-'ry where!

2. Old massa, he has heard it, don't it make him awful blue?
   Won't old Missus be a-ravin' when she finds it comin' true?
   'Specs there'll be a dreadful shakin', such as Jeffy cannot stand,
   'Cause kingdom come is a-movin' now, and a-clawin' through the land. *Chorus*

3. No more we'll work for nothin', but we'll own a little farm,
   And no more they'll sell our children, but we'll keep them from all harm;
   And no more we'll pick the cotton, and no more we'll feel the lash,
   We'll shout and drum on the old banjo, 'till we break it all to smash! *Chorus*

4. There'll be a big skedaddle, now old sixty-three has come!
   And the darkeys they will holler 'till they make the country hum.
   Oh, we thank Old Uncle Abra'm, yes, we bless him day and night,
   And pray the Lord bless the Union folks, and the battle for the right. *Chorus*

Grafted into the Army

"A rich man's war and a poor man's fight"—this was the cry taken up by the many who could not afford the $300 that it would take to buy an exemption from military service. Only about seven percent of the men whose names were drawn actually served. The bulk of the Union Army was made up of volunteers. So it was with some justice that a poor draftee might lament that he was "grafted" into the army.

Words and music by Henry C. Work

bar-my; I thought they would spare___ a lone wid-der's heir, But they

graft – ed him in – to the ar – my.

2. Dressed up in his unicorn, dear little chap,
   They have grafted him into the army;
   It seems but a day since he sot in my lap,
   But they grafted him into the army.
   And these are the trousies he used to wear,
   Them very same buttons, the patch and the tear;
   But Uncle Sam gave him a bran' new pair
   When they grafted him into the army. *Chorus*

3. Now in my provisions I see him revealed,
   They have grafted him into the army;
   A picket beside the contented field,
   They have grafted him into the army.
   He looks kinder sickish - begins to cry,
   A big volunteer standing right in his eye!
   Oh, what if the ducky should up and die,
   Now they've grafted him into the army. *Chorus*

Sambo's Right to Be Kilt

It was in his capacity as staff officer for General David Hunter that Charles Halpine ("Private Miles O'Reilly") helped prepare the order that mustered one of the first troops of black soldiers into the Union Army in 1862. This was a highly controversial policy, and Halpine chose satire to defend his superiors' actions.

Words by "Private Miles O'Reilly"
Music by S. Lover

Some tell me 'tis a burn-in' shame To make the nay-gers fight, And that the trade of be-in' kilt Be-longs but to the white. But as for me, up-

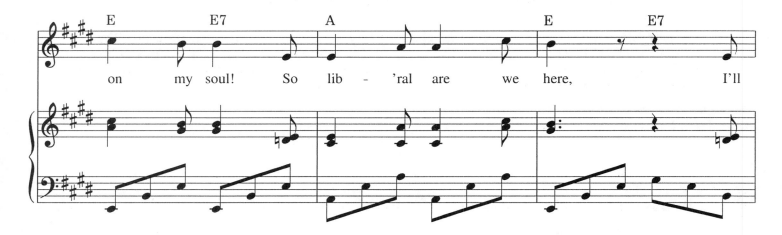

on my soul! So lib - 'ral are we here, I'll

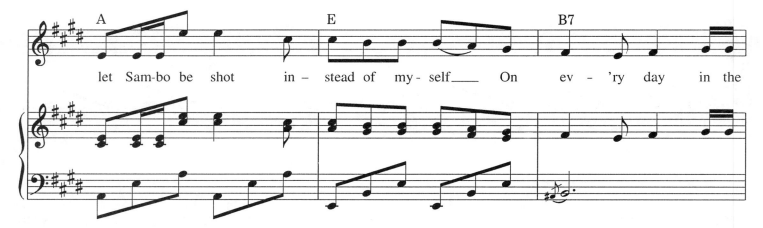

let Sam-bo be shot in - stead of my-self____ On ev - 'ry day in the

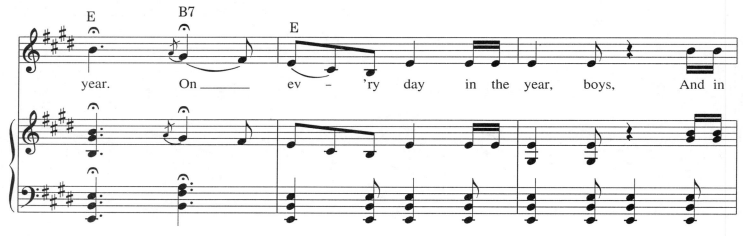

year. On ____ ev - 'ry day in the year, boys, And in

ev - 'ry hour in the day, The ____ right to be kilt I'll di -

vide ____ wid him, And ____ dev - il a word I'll say.

2. In battles wild commotion,
   I shouldn't at all object,
   If Sambo's body should stop a ball
   That's comin' for me direct;
   And the prod of a Southern bagnet*
   So ginerous are we here,
   I'll resign and let Sambo take it
   On every day in the year.
     On ev'ry day in the year, boys,
     And wid none 'iv your nasty pride,
     All my rights in a Southern bagnet prod,
     Wid Sambo I'll divide.

3. The men who object to Sambo
   Should take his place and fight;
   And it's better to have a nayger's hue
   Than a liver that's wake and white.
   Though Sambo's black as the ace of spades,
   His fingers a trigger can pull,
   And his eye runs straight on the barrel sight,
   From under the thatch of wool.
     On ev'ry day in the year, boys,
     Don't think that I'm tippin' you chaff,
     The right to be kilt we'll divide with him, boys,
     And give him the largest half.

   *Bayonet

Billy Barlow

Billy Barlow began life as an "I'm all right, Jack" sort of character in medieval England. He always managed to get the lion's share, due to fast talking and fast dealing. By the time the Civil War rolled around, he was firmly established on this side of the ocean as a well-known personage on stage and in song.

Words by Ed Clifford
Music: anonymous

Good eve-ning, kind friends, ___ how do you all do? ___ 'Tis a ver-y long time ___ since I've been to see you; I am a vol-un-teer, for the Un-ion I go; And I'm

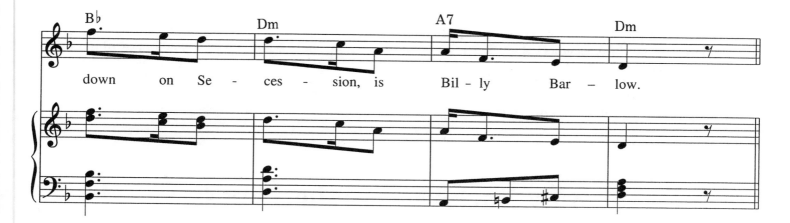

down on Se — ces — sion, is Bil — ly Bar — low.

Chorus

Oh! yes, I'm rough, I well know, But a

bul — ly old sol — dier is Bil — ly Bar — low.

2. Since last I saw you, to Richmond I've been;
  And during my stay, Mrs. Davis I've seen.
  She treated me kindly and smiled on me so...
  Old Jeff he got jealous of Billy Barlow.
    Oh! yes, I'm rough, I well know,
    But the ladies all like Mr. William Barlow.

3. Now the other night while out for a lark,
  I lost my way, it being quite dark;
  A sentinel grabbed me, to the guardhouse I did go.
  Oh! That was too rough on old Billy Barlow.
    Oh! yes, I'm rough, I well know,
    But they should not abuse old Billy Barlow.

4. Now I see on picket every time I go out,
  A nice little gal, her name is Lize Stout;
  They say she's Secesh, but I know that's not so;
  For she'll stand by the Union with Billy Barlow.
    Oh! yes, I'm rough, I well know,
    But a very good fellow is Billy Barlow.

5. Now, there's one thing I can't help but to look at –
  That is what keeps our Quartermaster so sleek and so fat;
  It may not be good living, but there's one thing I know:
  He'd get thin on the grub he gives Billy Barlow.
    Oh! yes, I'm rough, I well know,
    But I'm used to good living, is Billy Barlow.

6. It's down in Virginia, at a place called Bull Run,
Where first our brave soldiers their fighting begun;
It's true they got routed, but then you all know,
It was on account of the absence of Billy Barlow.
   Oh! yes, I'm rough, I well know,
   But a bully old soldier is Billy Barlow.

7. Just a few words more, then I shall have done,
And I hope what I've said, you'll take all in fun;
If I have not done right, why, please tell me so,
And I'll bid you good-night, will Billy Barlow.
   Oh! yes, I'm rough, I well know,
   But I hope you'll excuse poor old Billy Barlow.

Billy Barlow—On the Times

Words by H. Angelo
Music: "Billy Barlow"

1. I beg your attention, kind gentlefolks all,
I hope no intrusion in making this call;
It's been a long time since you've seen me, I know,
But I'm the identical Billy Barlow.
   Oh! dear, I'm ragged, I know,
   But the times have affected poor Billy Barlow.

2. Our country's excited 'bout this thing and that,
Both North and the South hardly know what they're at.
They secession, coercion, and compromise blow,
But it's talk and no cider, thinks Billy Barlow.
   Oh! dear, I'm ragged I know,
   But "Stand by the Union" will Billy Barlow.

3. If I had but the power I'd soon bring 'em to,
Though this may be nonsense I'm singing to you.
I'd hang of ringleaders a hundred or so,
And choke off secession, would Billy Barlow.
   Oh! dear, I'm ragged, I know,
   Then times would be better, thinks Billy Barlow.

4. Our cities are flooded with traitors and spies,
And our papers are filled with a strange pack of lies;
They'll agitate questions for friend or a foe,
Whilst they pocket the *rhino,* says Billy Barlow.
   Oh! dear, I'm ragged, I know,
   Self-interest they go for, thinks Billy Barlow.

5. Our members of Congress have plenty to do,
But it's seldom, if ever, they do it, 'tis true;
Political speeches for hours they'll blow,
But it all 'mounts to nothing, says Billy Barlow.
   Oh! dear, I'm ragged, I know,
   Why don't they do something? says Billy Barlow.

6. Believe me, my friend, in my song I don't err,
But the poor have to suffer when such things occur;
And as I belong to that class, you must know,
I'd fight for the Union, would Billy Barlow.
   Oh! dear, I'm ragged, I know,
   Hurrah for the Union! says Billy Barlow.

Kingdom Coming

(Year of Jubilo)

It was not uncommon for the most pro–Abolitionist and anti-slavery songs to be written and sung in pseudo–Negro "dialect." Whatever may be said today of the blackface performer in 19th century minstrel shows, he was a fixture of the American musical scene. This song was introduced with great fanfare in Chicago on April 23, 1862, by the famous Christy Minstrels. It was a rousing success, and was soon being sung and parodied all over the country (including the South).

Words and music by Henry C. Work

238

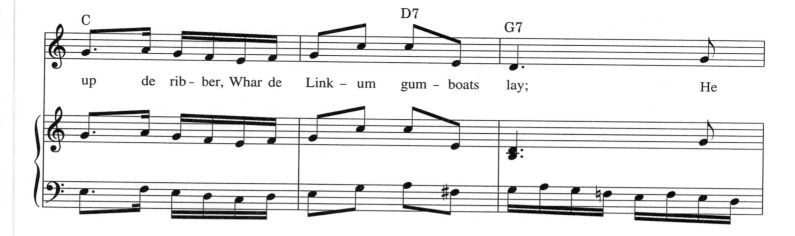

up de rib – ber, Whar de Link – um gum – boats lay;   He

took his hat, an lef' ber – ry sud – den, An' I spec' he's run a – way!   De

mas – sa run, ha, ha!   De dar – ky stay, ho, ho!   It

mus' be now de king – dom com – in', An' de year ob Ju – bi – lo!

2. He six foot one way, two foot tudder,
   An' he weigh tree hundred pound,
   His coat so big, he couldn't pay de tailor,
   An' it won't go half way 'round.
   He drill so much dey call him Cap'n,
   An' he got so drefful tanned,
   I spec' he try an' fool dem Yankees
   For to tink he's contraband. *Chorus*

3. De darkeys feel so lonesome libbing
   In de loghouse on de lawn,
   Dey move dar tings to massa's parlor
   For to keep it while he's gone.
   Dar's wine an' cider in de kitchen,
   An' de darkeys dey'll hab some;
   I spose day'll all be cornfiscated
   When de Linkum sojers come. *Chorus*

4. De oberseer he make us trouble,
   An' he dribe us 'round a spell;
   We lock him up in de smokehouse cellar,
   Wid de key trown in de well.
   De whip is lost, de han'cuff broken,
   But de massa'll hab his pay;
   He's ole enough, big enough, ought to known better
   Dan to went an' run away. *Chorus*

Babylon Is Fallen

Here again we find a "well-intentioned" white composer's attempt at conveying his impression of black speech in what is obviously a fervently pro—emancipation song.

Words and music by Henry C. Work

out dar, now! We's a-gwine to shoot! Look out dar, don't you un-der-

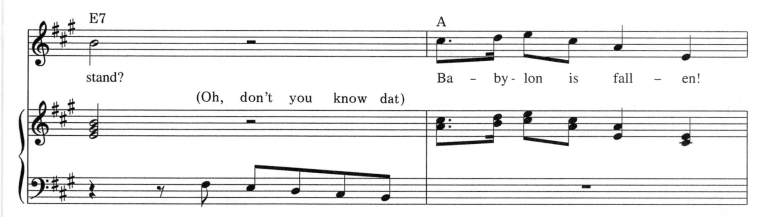

stand? (Oh, don't you know dat) Ba - by-lon is fall – en!

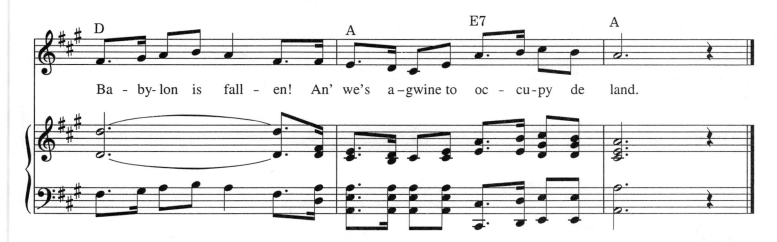

Ba - by-lon is fall – en! An' we's a-gwine to oc - cu-py de land.

2. Don't you see de lightnin'
   Flashin' in de canebrake,
   Like as if we's gwine to hab a storm?
   No! You is mistaken,
   'Tis de darkies' bay'nets,
   An' de buttons on dar uniform. *Chorus*

3. Way up in de cornfield,
   Whar you hear de tunder,
   Dat is our ole forty-pounder gun;
   When de shells are missin',
   Den we load wid punkins,
   All de same to make de cowards run. *Chorus*

4. Massa was de Kernel
   In de Rebel army,
   Eber sence he went an' run away;
   But his lubly darkies,
   Dey has been a-watchin',
   An' dey take him pris'ner tudder day. *Chorus*

5. We will be de Massa,
   He will be de sarvant,
   Try him how he like it for a spell;
   So we crack de Butt'nuts,
   So we take de Kernel,
   So de cannon carry back de shell. *Chorus*

De Day ob Liberty's Comin'

It is interesting to note that George Root used the *nom de plume* "Wurzel" on the sheet music of his comic and dialect songs. "Wurzel" in German means "root," and after the blackface performer, the most often stereotyped comic figure was the so-called "Dutchman," the heavily accented German immigrant. We shall meet one of these characters on page 248.

Words and music by George F. Root

Loud! loud! dar voic - es ring, Good news de

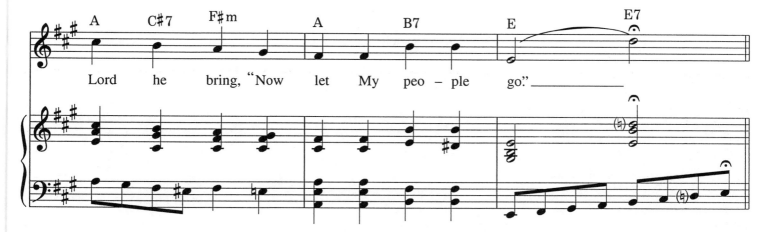

Lord he bring, "Now let My peo – ple go." _____

Chorus

Just you look and see __ dat __ light! De day ob lib- er- ty's com- in', com- in',

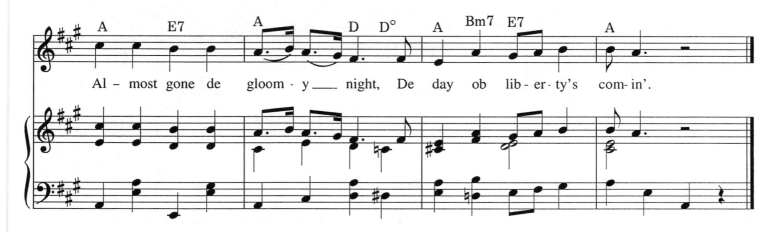

Al – most gone de gloom- y __ night, De day ob lib- er- ty's com- in'.

2. De Union folks dey wait so long,
   We tink dey neber was comin', comin',
   And Secesh he get so strong,
   We tink dey neber was comin'.
   Now Uncle Abe he say,
   Come massa while you may,
   And for de slabe we'll pay,
   For we must let him go. *Chorus*

3. White folks let us help ye trou,
   De day ob liberty's comin', comin',
   We can fight and die for you,
   De day ob liberty's comin'.
   Yes! yes! we'll shout and sing,
   Loud! loud! our voices ring,
   Soon! soon! de mighty King
   Will let His people go. *Chorus*

4. O de Lord will bring it right,
   De day ob liberty's comin', comin',
   From dis drefful bloody fight,
   De day ob liberty's comin'.
   Shout! darkeys, shout and sing,
   Loud let your voices ring,
   Soon! soon! de mighty King,
   Will let His people go. *Chorus*

I Goes to Fight mit Sigel

Franz Sigel, a German refugee from the Revolution of 1848, was appointed major general by Lincoln in an attempt to convince the large German-born northern population that this war was their war, too. Professional Union officers felt that "It seems but little better than murder to give important commands to such men as…Sigel…yet it seems impossible to prevent it." While not all "political generals" fared badly, in Sigel's case the criticism was well taken; he was a rather ineffective leader, despite the enthusiastic lyrics written by F. Poole (almost invariably dialect songs were written by composers of different ethnic groups from the ones depicted in their songs).

Words by F. Poole
Music: "The Girl I Left Behind Me"

I've come shust now to tells__ you how I goes mit re - gi - men - tals, To__ schlauch dem voes of Lib - er - ty, Like dem old Con ti - nen - tals, Vot__

fights mit Eng–land long a-go, To__ save der Yan-kee Ea – gle; Und__

now I gets my sol – dier__clothes, I goes to fight mit__ Si – gel.

2. Ven I comes from der Deutsche Countree,
   I vorks somedimes at baking;
   Den I keeps a lager beer saloon,
   Und den I goes shoemaking;
   But now I vas a sojer been
   To save der Yankee Eagle,
   To schlauch dem tam secession volks,
   I goes to fight mit Sigel.

3. I gets ein tam big rifle guns,
   Und puts him to mine shoulder,
   Den march so bold like a big jackhorse,
   Und may been someding bolder;
   I goes off mit de volunteers
   To save der Yankee Eagle;
   To give dem Rebel vellers fits,
   I goes to fight mit Sigel.

4. Dem Deutschen mens mit Sigel's band
   At fighting have no rival;
   Und ven Cheff Davis mens ve meet,
   Ve schlauch em like de tuyvil.
   Dere's only von ting vot I fear,
   Ven pattling for der Eagle,
   I vont get not no lager beer,
   Ven I goes to fight mit Sigel.

5. For rations dey gives salty pork,
   I dinks dat vas a great sell;
   I petter likes de sauerkraut,
   Der Schvitzer-kase und bretzel.
   If Fighting Joe will give us dem,
   Ve'll save der Yankee Eagle,
   Und I'll put mine vrou in breech-a-loons,
   To go and fight mit Sigel.

The Grant Pill

"No terms except an unconditional and immediate surrender can be accepted." (Grant's reply to Confederate General Buckner at Fort Donelson, Tennessee, February 16, 1862.)

Words by Harriet L. Castle
Music by J. C. Beckel

You see, my jol – ly com – rades, we are ripe and prime for bat – tle; We

heed – ed not the can – non's roar nor grape shot's his – sing rat – tle. We were

sworn to death or vic – t'ry for our Un – ion, God de – fend her; And to

2. Amidst the din of warfare and the shrieks of hosts a-dying,
   We heard a shout of triumph, saw the flag of truce a-flying;
   And we knew the rebel leader a petition came to tender,
   But our gallant General *Granted* unconditional surrender. *Chorus*

3. " 'Tis unchivalric treatment to a man in my condition,
   But I yield me," said their leader, so our armies gained admission.
   Then our flag went up instanter as she must, when braves defend her,
   And while leaders have this war cry: "Unconditional surrender!" *Chorus*

4. Hurrah! then for our Union, our Flag and Constitution;
   While we've hands and hearts for battle we will have no dissolution.
   Hurrah! then for our Union, peace and liberty attend her;
   And henceforth be this our war cry: "Unconditional surrender!" *Chorus*

Richmond Is a Hard Road to Travel

Union General Ambrose E. Burnside—whose flamboyant side-whiskers were first known as "burnsides" and now as "sideburns"—was the butt of this 1863 satire. Apparently, Southern satirists were not the only ones who held Burnside up to scorn. Once, when Lincoln was informed that a dispatch from Burnside had been received, to the effect that defeat and surrender were practically upon him, the President remarked: "I am glad of it; I am glad to hear it." When his aide wondered at Lincoln's strange reaction, the following explanation was offered:

"Well, it reminds me of a poor woman I used to know.... She had a large brood of children. They wandered through the woods, and it was impossible for her to clothe them properly— she could hardly feed them. The woman always used to say that it did her heart good whenever any of those young ones came around squalling, because then she knew he was still alive."

Words: anonymous
Music "Jordan Is a Hard Road to Travel" (by Daniel D. Emmett)

slips, And the ver – y lat – est burst – ing of the bub – ble?
shore, That Rich – mond was a hard road to trav – el.

Chorus

Then pull off your coat and roll ___ up your sleeve, For

Rich – mond is a hard road to trav – el; Then

pull off your coat and roll ___ up your sleeve, For

Rich - mond is a hard road to trav - el, I be – lieve!

2. First, McDowell, bold and gay, set forth the shortest way,
   By Manassas in the pleasant summer weather,
   But unfortunately ran on a Stonewall, foolish man,
   And had a "rocky journey" altogether;
   And he found it rather hard to ride o'er Beauregard,
   And Johnston proved a deuce of a bother,
   And 'twas clear beyond a doubt that he didn't like the route,
   And a second time would have to try another.
     Then pull off your coat and roll up your sleeve,
     For Manassas is a hard road to travel;
     Manassas gave us fits, and Bull Run made us grieve,
     For Richmond is a hard road to travel, I believe!

3. Next came the Wooly-Horse,* with an overwhelming force,
   To march down to Richmond by the Valley,
   But he couldn't find the road, and his "onward movement" showed
   His campaigning was a mere shilly-shally.
   Then Commissary Banks, with his motley foreign ranks,
   Kicking up a great noise, fuss, and flurry,
   Lost the whole of his supplies, and with tears in his eyes,
   From the Stonewall ran away in a hurry.
     Then pull off your coat and roll up your sleeve,
     For the Valley is a hard road to travel;
     The Balley wouldn't do and we all had to leave,
     For Richmond is a hard road to travel, I believe!

4. Then the great *Galena* came, with her portholes all aflame,
   And the *Monitor,* that famous naval wonder,
   But the guns at Drury's Bluff gave them speedily enough,
   The loudest sort of reg'lar Rebel thunder.
   The *Galena* was astonished and the *Monitor* admonished,
   Our patent shot and shell were mocked at,
   While the dreadful *Naugatuck,* by the hardest kind of luck,
   Was knocked into an ugly cocked hat.
     Then pull off your coat and roll up your sleeve,
     For James River is a hard road to travel;
     The gun-boats gave it up in terror and despair,
     For Richmond is a hard road to travel, I declare!

*General Fremont

5. Then McClellan followed soon, both with spade and balloon,
   To try the Peninsular approaches,
   But one and all agreed that his best rate of speed
   Was no faster than the slowest of "slow coaches."
   Instead of easy ground, at Williamsburg he found
   A *Longstreet* indeed, and nothing shorter,
   And it put him in the dumps, that spades wasn't trumps,
   And the *Hills* he couldn't level "as he orter."
     Then pull off your coat and roll up your sleeve,
     For *Longstreet* is a hard road to travel;
     Lay down the shovel, and throw away the spade,
     For Richmond is a hard road to travel, I'm afraid!

6. Then said Lincoln unto Pope, "You can make the trip, I hope –
   I will save the Universal Yankee nation,
   To make sure of no defeat, I'll leave no lines of retreat,
   And issue a famous proclamation."
   But that same dreaded Jackson, this fellow laid his whacks on,
   And made him, by compulsion, a *seceder.* *
   And Pope took rapid flight from Manassas' second fight,
   'Twas his very last appearance as a leader.
     Then pull off your coat and roll up your sleeve,
     For *Stonewall* is a hard road to travel;
     Pope did his very best, but was evidently sold,
     For Richmond is a hard road to travel, I am told!

7. Last of all the *brave* Burnside, with his pontoon bridges, tried
   A road no one had thought of before him,
   With two hundred thousand men for the Rebel slaughter pen,
   And the blessed Union flag waving o'er him;
   But he met a fire like hell, of canister and shell,
   That mowed his men down with great slaughter,
   'Twas a shocking sight to view, that second Waterloo,
   And the river ran with more blood than water.
     Then pull off your coat and roll up your sleeve,
     Rappahannock is a hard road to travel;
     Burnside got in a trap, which caused him for to grieve,
     For Richmond is a hard road to travel, I believe!

8. We are very much perplexed to know who is the next
   To command the new Richmond expedition,
   For the Capital must blaze, and that in ninety days,
   And Jeff and his men be sent to perdition.
   We'll take the cursed town, and then we'll burn it down,
   And plunder and hang up each cursed Rebel;
   Yet the contraband was right when he told us they would fight,
   "Oh, yes, massa, they fight like the devil!"
     Then pull off your coat roll up your sleeve,
     For Richmond is a hard road to travel;
   Then pull off your coat and roll up your sleeve,
   For Richmond is a hard road to travel, I believe!

*The Battle of Cedar Run

Overtures from Richmond

In 1687, English composer Henry Purcell wrote this melody, which throughout the years has served as a vehicle for numerous sets of lyrics. Professor Francis James Child, renowned for his monumental study of Anglo–American folk songs, *The English and Scottish Popular Ballads,* added his own contribution to this reworking of Purcell's melody.

Words by Francis J. Child
Music: "Lilliburlero"

With broad humor ♩ = 168

"Well, Un–cle Sam," says Jef – fer–son D., Lil – li – bur – le – ro, old Un–cle Sam, "You'll have to join my Con – fed'–ra – cy," Lil – li – bur – le – ro, old Un–cle Sam.

2. "So, Uncle Sam, just lay down your arms,"
   Lilliburlero, old Uncle Sam,
  "Then you shall hear my reas'nable terms,"
   Lilliburlero, old Uncle Sam.
  "Lero, lero, I'd like to hear-o
  I'd like to hear," says old Uncle Sam,
  "Lero, lero, filibuster-o,
  I'd like to hear," says old Uncle Sam.

3. "First you must own I've beat you in fight,"
   Lilliburlero, old Uncle Sam,
  "Then that I always have been in the right,"
   Lilliburlero, old Uncle Sam.
  "Lero, lero, rather severe-o
  Rather severe," says old Uncle Sam.
  "Lero, lero, filibuster-o,
  Rather severe," says old Uncle Sam.

4. "Then you must pay my national debts,"
   Lilliburlero, old Uncle Sam,
   "No questions asked about my assets,"
   Lilliburlero, old Uncle Sam.
   "Lero, lero, that's very dear-o
   That's very dear," says old Uncle Sam,
   "Lero, lero, filibuster-o,
   That's very dear," says old Uncle Sam.

5. "Also some few IOU's and bets,"
   Lilliburlero, old Uncle Sam,
   "Mine, and Bob Toombs,' and Sidell's and Rhett's,"
   Lilliburlero, old Uncle Sam.
   "Lero, lero, that leaves me zero,
   That leaves me zero," says Uncle Sam,
   "Lero, lero, filibuster-o,
   That leaves me zero," says Uncle Sam.

6. "And by the way, one little thing more,"
   Lilliburlero, old Uncle Sam,
   "You're to refund the costs of the war,"
   Lilliburlero, old Uncle Sam.
   "Lero, lero, just what I fear-o,
   Just what I fear," says old Uncle Sam,
   "Lero, lero, filibuster-o,
   Just what I fear," says old Uncle Sam.

7. "Next, you must own our Cavalier blood!"
   Lilliburlero, old Uncle Sam,
   "And that your Puritans sprang from the mud!"
   Lilliburlero, old Uncle Sam.
   "Lero, lero, that mud is clear-o,
   That mud is clear," says old Uncle Sam.
   "Lero, lero, filibuster-o,
   That mud is clear," says old Uncle Sam.

8. "Slavery's, of course, the chief corner-stone,"
   Lilliburlero, old Uncle Sam,
   "Of our new civ-il-i-za-tion!"
   Lilliburlero, old Uncle Sam.
   "Lero, lero, that's quite sincere-o,
   That's quite sincere," says old Uncle Sam,
   "Lero, lero, filibuster-o,
   That's quite sincere," says old Uncle Sam.

9. "You'll understand, my recreant tool,"
   Lilliburlero, old Uncle Sam,
   "You're to submit, and we are to rule,"
   Lilliburlero, old Uncle Sam.
   "Lero, lero, aren't you a hero!
   Aren't you a hero," says Uncle Sam,
   "Lero, lero, filibuster-o,
   Aren't you a hero," says Uncle Sam.

10. "If to these terms you fully consent,"
    Lilliburlero, old Uncle Sam,
    "I'll be Perpetual King-President,"
    Lilliburlero, old Uncle Sam.
    "Lero, lero, take your sombrero,
    Off to your swamps," says old Uncle Sam,
    "Lero, lero, filibuster-o,
    Cut, double quick!" says old Uncle Sam.

High-Toned Southern Gentleman

Another old English song, borrowed and reworked to fit a new set of circumstances. A notation referring to the "song of the 'Old Courtier of Queen Elizabeth' and how he was changed" is to be found in Pepys' diary (June 16, 1688).

Words: anonymous
Music: "Fine Old English Gentleman"

Down in the sun – ny South – ern clime, the cu – rious ones may find, A

rip – ping, tear – ing gen – tle – man of an un – com – mon kind,   A

stag – g'ring, swag – g'ring sort of chap, that takes his whis – ky straight,   And

fre – quent–ly con – demns his eyes un – to an aw – ful fate, A

high – toned South–ern gen – tle–man, one of the pres – ent time.

2. He always wears a full dress coat, pre–Adamite in cut,
   With waistcoat of the broadest style, through which his ruffles jut;
   Six breastpins deck his horrid front, and on his fingers shine
   Whole invoices of diamond rings, *which would hardly pass muster with the "Original Jacobs" in Chatham Street*
      for jewels genuine;
   This "high-toned Southern gentleman," one of the present time.

3. He takes to euchre kindly, too, and plays an awful hand,
   Especially when those he tricks his style don't understand,
   And if he wins, why then he stops to pocket all the stakes,
   But if he loses, then he says *to the unfortunate stranger who had chanced to win, "It's my opinion you are a
      cursed Abolitionist, and if you don't leave South Carolina in an hour, you'll be hung like a dog!" but no offer* to
      pay his losses makes;
   This "high-toned Southern gentleman," one of the present time.

4. Of course, he's all the time in debt to those who credit give,
   Yet manages upon the best the market yields to live;
   But if a Northern creditor asks him his bill to heed,
   This honorable gentleman *instantly draws his bowie knife and pistols, dons a blue cockade, and declares that, in
      consequence of the repeated aggressions of the North and its gross violations of the Constitution, he feels that it
      would utterly degrade him to pay any debt whatever, and in fact that he has at last* determined to SECEDE!
   This "high-toned Southern gentleman," one of the present time.

Note: Italicized words should be chanted in a monotone at an increasing tempo.

Hard Times in Dixie

One day toward the end of the war, a weary and worn-out Confederate soldier sat cooling his feet in a stream, while with a rusty needle and coarse thread he was endeavoring to mend his ragged coat. Suddenly a mounted Federal dashed into view and, riding rapidly toward the Confederate, he shouted, "Hi, there, Johnny Reb. I've got you this time." Without looking up from his mending, the half-starved, ragged, and dirty fellow replied, "Yes, and a hell of a git you got."

Words by M. K.
Music by Eugarps

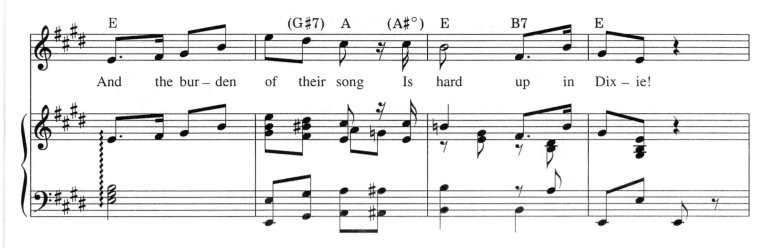

And the bur – den of their song Is hard up in Dix – ie!

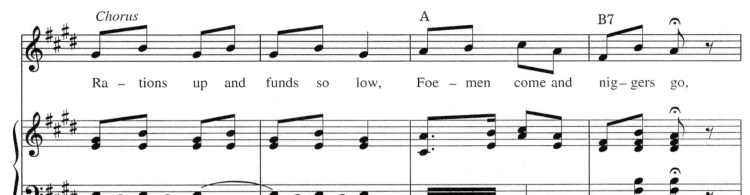

Chorus

Ra – tions up and funds so low, Foe – men come and nig – gers go,

Worst of all the Yank – ees know, We're hard up in Dix – ie.

2. Grant is close upon their track,
   It's hard times in Dixie!
   Southern fire won't turn him back,
   Hard times in Dixie.
     With his Heroes tested well,
     What cares he for shot or shell,
     Southern brag or Southern swell —
     They're hard up in Dixie! *Chorus*

3. Uncle Abe don't flinch a bit
   For hard times in Dixie!
   Though as any rail he's split,
   Hard up in Dixie;
     Holding out his honest hands,
     Welcoming all *loyal* bands,
     Abraham well understands
     They're hard up in Dixie! *Chorus*

4. Butler, with his soldiers true,
   Makes hard times in Dixie!
   When he came the Rebels knew
   Hard times in Dixie!
     Johnny Rebs don't see the fun,
     Want begins and credit's done,
     White man works and darkey runs,
     They're hard up in Dixie! *Chorus*

5. Beat the drum and toll the bell,
   For hard times in Dixie!
   Chant Rebellion's funeral knell —
   Hard times in Dixie!
     And while over land and sea,
     Floats the banner of the free,
     Traitors shall forever be
     Hard up in Dixie! *Chorus*

263

Jeff in Petticoats

"I stepped out of my wife's tent and saw some horsemen…cavalry…regular troopers…. As it was quite dark…I picked up what was supposed to be my 'raglan'…it was subsequently found out to be my wife's…as I started, my wife thoughtfully threw over my head and shoulders a shawl. I had gone perhaps fifteen or twenty yards when a trooper galloped up and ordered me to halt and surrender…." [*Jefferson Davis attempting to explain why he was dressed in his wife's clothing when captured (May 10, 1865) in* **Abraham Lincoln: A History** *(New York, 1890)*]

Words by Henry Tucker
Music by George Cooper

spanked him well, and that's the end Of brave old Jef – fy D.

Chorus

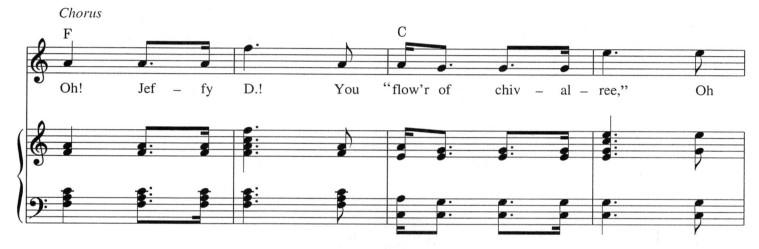

Oh! Jef – fy D.! You "flow'r of chiv – al – ree," Oh

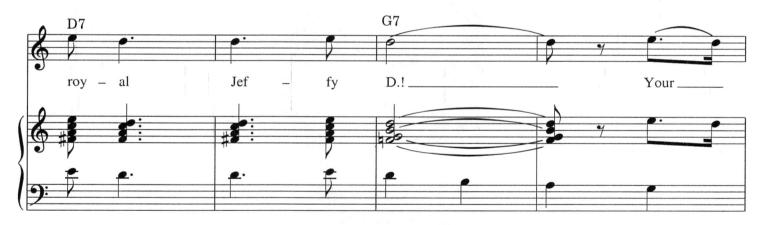

roy – al Jef – fy D.! _____ Your _____

em – pire's but a tin – clad skirt, Oh, charm – ing Jef – fy D.

2. This Davis, he was always full
   Of bluster and of brag,
   He swore, on all our Northern walls,
   He'd plant his Rebel rag;
   But when to battle he did go,
   He said, "I'm not so green,
   To dodge the bullets, I will wear
   My tin-clad crinoline." *Chorus*

3. Now when he saw the game was up,
   He started for the woods,
   His bandbox hung upon his arm
   Quite full of fancy goods;
   Said Jeff, "They'll never take me now,
   I'm sure I'll not be seen.
   They'd never think to look for me
   Beneath my crinoline." *Chorus*

4. Jeff took with him, the people say,
   A mine of golden coin,
   Which he, from banks and other places,
   Managed to purloin;
   But while he ran, like every thief,
   He had to drop the spoons,
   And maybe that's the reason why
   He dropped his pantaloons. *Chorus*

5. Our Union boys were on his track
   For many nights and days,
   His palpitating heart it beat,
   Enough to burst his stays;
   Oh! what a dash he must have cut
   With form so tall and lean;
   Just fancy now the "What is it?"
   Dressed up in crinoline! *Chorus*

6. The ditch that Jeff was hunting for,
   He found was very near;
   He tried to "shift" his base again,
   His neck felt rather queer;
   Just on the out-"skirts" of a wood
   His dainty shape was seen,
   His boots stuck out, and now they'll hang
   Old Jeff in crinoline. *Chorus*

Post Bellum

Oh, I'm a Good Old Rebel

At Appomattox a Union soldier tried to lighten the mood when he bade farewell to a dispirited Confederate. "Well, Johnny, I guess you fellows will go home now to stay." The bedraggled Southerner was in no mood for playful small talk, and retorted, "Look here, Yank; you *guess*, do you that we fellows are going home to stay? Maybe we are. But don't be giving us any of your impudence. If you do we'll come back and lick you again."

Words ascribed to Major Innes Randolph, C.S.A.
Music: "Joe Bowers"

Oh, I'm a good old Reb - el, Now that's just what I am, For
this "Fair Land of Free - dom" I do not give a damn! I'm
gald I fit a - gainst it, I on - ly wish we'd won, And

I don't want no par – don For an – y – thing I done. _____

2. I hates the Constitution,
   This Great Republic, too,
   I hates the Freedman's Buro,
   In uniforms of blue;
   I hates the nasty eagle,
   With all his brag and fuss,
   The lyin', thievin' Yankees,
   I hates 'em wuss and wuss.

3. I hates the Yankee nation
   And everything they do,
   I hates the Declaration
   Of Independence, too;
   I hates the "glorious Union,"
   'Tis dripping with our blood,
   I hates their striped banner,
   I fit it all I could.

4. I followed old Marse Robert
   For four year, near about,
   Got wounded in three places
   And starved at P'int Lookout;
   I cotch the "roomatism,"
   A-campin' in the snow,
   But I killed a chance o' Yankees,
   I'd like to kill some mo'.

5. Three hundred thousand Yankees
   Is stiff in Southern dust;
   We got three hundred thousand
   Before they conquered us;
   They died of Southern fever
   And Southern steel and shot,
   I wish they was three million
   Instead of what we got.

6. I can't take up my musket
   And fight 'em now no more,
   But I ain't a-going to love 'em,
   Now that is sarten sure;
   And I don't want no pardon
   For what I was and am,
   I won't be reconstructed
   And I don't care a damn!

The Blue and the Gray

"I remember," said one grizzled Confederate veteran to another, "when we pushed them damnyankees all the way across the Ohio and up into Illinois!" The other old-timer shook his head and said, "That wasn't exactly the way it happened. I was there. Those Yankees drove *us* out of Paducah and almost to the Tennessee line." The first veteran thought it over a bit and then muttered, "Another good story ruined by an eye witness!"

Words by M. F. Finch
Music by Felix Schelling

By the flow of the in – land __ riv – er, Where the fleet of __ i – ron has fled, Where the blades of the grave grass quiv – er, A – sleep are the ranks of the dead. Un – der the sod and the